FHA

Training Manual for Loan Officers and Loan Processors

BRIAN L. CRISWEL

MTG Book Company also publishes its books in electronic format. Some content that appears in print may not be available in electronic books.

Printed in the United States of America

briancriswel@gmail.com

BRIAN L. CRISWEL

FHA

Training Manual for Loan Officers and Loan Processors

Author
Brian L. Criswel

Contributing Editors
John Forsyth
Clarissa Dunaldson
Cathy L. Stephens

Proofreading and Typesetting
Brian Tubbin
Jessica Thompkins
Maurice Goodwell

Editors
Reginald Wallace
Tammatha Woodruff
Gary P. Scott

Production Planners
McKenna Roberts
Carla Hodges
Tameka Ellis

Cover Design
Alfreda Woods

Research
Alexander Reynolds

CONTENTS

CHAPTER 3: Maximum Mortgage Amounts and Cash Investment Requirements on Purchase Transactions 41

CHAPTER 4: Refinance Transaction Overview 57

CHAPTER 5: Borrower Eligibility and Credit Analysis   67

CHAPTER 7: Special Underwriting   137

Federal Housing Administration Overview

The Federal Housing Administration, also known as "FHA", was started in 1934. FHA insures mortgage loans made by approved lenders in the United States and US territories. FHA has insured over 30 million properties since its inception and is considered the largest insurer of mortgages in the world.

Shortly before FHA was started the housing industry in the United States was experiencing a great deal of turmoil. Unemployment was high and mortgage loan terms were difficult to meet, leaving many individuals and families unable to achieve the American Dream of home ownership.

Before FHA was started:

- Only 4 in 10 households owned.
- Dwellings in the U.S. were occupied primarily by renters.
- LTV was limited to 50%.
- Loan terms were 36 to 60 months (then balloon payments were due).

What is FHA Mortgage Insurance?

FHA mortgage insurance is simply a guarantee by the U.S. government that in the case a borrower defaults on an FHA backed loan the lender's losses would be covered and a "claim" would be paid to the lender in the amount not covered by foreclosure proceedings. Because the risk in this type of transaction lays squarely on the shoulders of FHA, the guidelines are set by FHA and must be strictly adhered to by lenders seeking FHA mortgage insurance in order to qualify.

How is FHA funded?

Though the FHA is a government agency its operating costs are not covered through taxpayer dollars, it's a completely self-supporting agency, through mortgage insurance premiums paid by the borrowers of FHA-insured loans.

Does FHA make mortgage loans, like a lender?

No. FHA does not directly make mortgage loans. FHA insures approved lenders against losses on mortgage loans.

Housing & Urban Development (HUD) Overview

HUD is an acronym standing for Housing and Urban Development, a cabinet of the United States. It has existed since 1965 and is charged with ensuring smooth policy for housing and city development. Since the mid-1970s, its focus has shifted primarily to housing, leaving urban planning more in the hands of individual cities.

One of the main functions of HUD, and certainly that with which most people interact, is its role as a lending facilitator. HUD helps people of low- and mid-level incomes acquire loans to purchase housing. HUD itself is not a lending institution, but it approves lenders and supports them materially. HUD also offers extensive counseling services for potential homeowners. A network exists through HUD of organizations which address key educational issues relating to home ownership. HUD funds special programs through grants, all with the aim of assisting Americans who wish to buy a house. In addition to counsel relating to first-time purchases, HUD also supports organizations which offer advice on foreclosure, defaults, renting and many credit issues.

HUD's areas of assistance are not confined to those listed above; virtually anything relating to home-ownership or rental falls within the jurisdiction of HUD. This includes safety issues, housing discrimination, senior housing, home repair and homeowner's insurance.

HUD is also loosely connected to the the Federal Home Loan Mortgage Corporation (Freddie Mac) and the Federal National Mortgage Association (Fannie Mae), both of which deal with mortgages in the United States. The Federal Housing Administration (FHA) falls more closely under HUD, helping to guarantee mortgages to low-income homeowners.

Home Ownership Centers

HOC - Home Ownership Centers - HUD has consolidated the various local HUD Field Offices into four (4) Home Ownership Centers (HOCs) which are organized to serve specific states. These HOCs are responsible for the policies and procedures that lenders are responsible for applying to the origination, processing, underwriting, closing and insuring of FHA loans.

ATLANTA HOC	Alabama Indiana North Carolina Virgin Islands	Florida Indiana Puerto Rico Georgia	Kentucky South Carolina Illinois Mississippi	Tennessee
PHILADELPHIA HOC	Connecticut Maryland New Jersey New York Vermont	Delaware Massachusetts New York Ohio Virginia	Washington, DC Michigan Ohio Pennsylvania West Virginia	Maine New Hampshire New Jersey Rhode Island
DENVER HOC	Arkansas Louisiana Nebraska South Dakota Wyoming	Colorado Minnesota New Mexico Texas	Iowa Missouri North Dakota Utah	Kansas Montana Oklahoma Wisconsin
SANTA ANA HOC	Alaska Hawaii Washington	Arizona Idaho California	Nevada Guam Oregon	

Atlanta Homeownership Center

Homeownership Centers insure single family FHA mortgages and oversee the selling of HUD homes. The Atlanta Homeownership Center serves the states of Alabama, Florida, Georgia, Kentucky, Illinois, Indiana, Mississippi, North Carolina, South Carolina, and Tennessee, as well as the Caribbean.

> U.S. Department of Housing and Urban Development
> Atlanta Homeownership Center
> Five Points Plaza
> 40 Marietta Street
> Atlanta, GA 30303-2806
> Telephone: (800) CALL-FHA (800-225-5342)
> 1-888-696-4687

ATLHOC Addresses:	
All ATLHOC general mail and casebinders: U.S. Dept. of HUD Atlanta Homeownership Center 40 Marietta Street Atlanta, GA 30303-2806 Attn: Insuring	**All ATLHOC MIC correction requests:** DHUD - Atlanta Homeownership Center Five Points Plaza 40 Marietta Street Atlanta, GA 30303-2806 Attn: MIC Corrections
All ATLHOC non profit program documents: U.S. Dept. of HUD ATLHOC Non-profit Team 40 Marietta Street Atlanta, GA 30303-2806 Attn: Program Support Division	**All ATLHOC downpayment assistance program documents:** U.S. Dept. of HUD Atlanta Homeownership Center 40 Marietta Street Atlanta, GA 30303-2806 Attn: Program Support Division
All ATLHOC mortgage limit increase documents: U.S. Dept. of HUD Atlanta Homeownership Center 40 Marietta Street Atlanta, GA 30303-2806 Attn: Program Support Division	**All ATLHOC Housing counseling packages:** U.S. Dept. of HUD Atlanta Homeownership Center 40 Marietta Street Atlanta, GA 30303-2806 Attn: Program Support Division

Philadelphia Homeownership Center

HUD Homeownership Centers insure single family FHA mortgages and oversee the selling of HUD homes. The Philadelphia Homeownership Center serves the states of Connecticut, Delaware, District of Columbia, Maine, Maryland, Massachusetts, Michigan, New Hampshire, New Jersey, New York, Ohio, Pennsylvania, Rhode Island, Vermont, Virginia, West Virginia.

> U.S. Department of Housing and Urban Development
> Philadelphia Homeownership Center
> The Wanamaker Building
> 100 Penn Square East
> Philadelphia, PA 19107-3389
> Telephone: (800) CALL-FHA (800-225-5342)

Denver Homeownership Center

HUD Homeownership Centers insure single family FHA mortgages and oversee the selling of HUD homes. The Denver Homeownership Center serves the states of Arkansas, Colorado, Iowa, Kansas, Louisiana, Missouri, Minnesota, Montana, Nebraska, New Mexico, North Dakota, Oklahoma, South Dakota, Texas, Wisconsin, Wyoming, and Utah. Telephone: (800) CALL-FHA.

DENHOC Addresses:	
Case Binders : US Dept. of HUD Denver Homeownership Center Processing & Underwriting - 20th FL 1670 Broadway Denver, Co. 80202	**Program Support Division Mail:** DHUD Denver Homeownership Center Program Support Division - 21st Floor 1670 Broadway Denver, CO 80202-4801
Condominium Approval Requests **Office of Single Family:** U. S. Department of Housing and Urban Development Denver Homeownership Center Attn: Technical Support Branch, 21st Floor 1670 Broadway Denver, CO 80202	**Mortgage Limit Requests:** Fargo Field Office DHUD 657 2nd Ave North 3rd Floor, Room 366 P.O. Box 2483 Fargo, ND 58102-2483
General Mail: U.S. Department of Housing and Urban Development Denver Homeownership Center UMB Plaza Building 1670 Broadway Denver, CO 80202-4801	

Santa Ana Homeownership Center

HUD Homeownership Centers insure single family FHA mortgages, assure FHA mortgage quality, help homeowners & homebuyers through effective housing counseling, & oversee the selling of HUD homes. The Santa Ana Homeownership Center (SAHOC) serves the states of Alaska, Arizona, California, Hawaii, Idaho, Nevada, Oregon and Washington. We also serve the Pacific Islands of American Samoa, Guam, & the Commonwealth of the Northern Marianas. (800-225-5342)

SAHOC Addresses:	
All SAHOC general mail and casebinders: U.S. Department of Housing & Urban Development Santa Ana Homeownership Center Santa Ana Federal Building 34 Civic Center Plaza, Room 7015 Santa Ana, CA 92701-4003	All SAHOC Non-profit Program Documents & Downpayment Assistance Program (DAP) Documents: U.S. Department of Housing & Urban Development 6245 E. Broadway Blvd., Suite 350 Tucson, AZ 85711 Attn: SAHOC Non-profit Team

CHAPTER ONE

Loan Origination Requirements/Restrictions

1. Overview of FHA Single Family Mortgage Insurance Programs

a. Purpose of FHA Mortgage Insurance Programs

The Federal Housing Administration (FHA) offers various mortgage insurance programs, under which they insure approved lenders against losses on mortgage loans. FHA-insured mortgages may be used to purchase homes, improve homes, and to refinance existing mortgages.

b. What FHA Will and Will Not Insure

FHA's programs differ from one another primarily in terms of what types of properties and financing are eligible. Except as otherwise stated in this handbook, FHA's single family programs are limited to one to four unit properties that are owner-occupied principal residences only. FHA insures mortgages on properties that consist of:

- detached or semi-detached dwellings
- townhouses or row houses, or
- individual units with FHA-approved condominium projects.

FHA will <u>NOT</u> insure mortgages on:
- commercial enterprises
- hotels and motels
- bed and breakfast establishments
- fraternity and sorority houses
- boarding houses
- tourist houses
- private clubs

c. Direct Endorsement Program

Under FHA's DE program, approved lenders may underwrite and close mortgage loans without prior FHA review or approval. This includes all aspects of the mortgage loan application, the property analysis, and borrower underwriting.

Note: This assumes that the lender is a DE lender with unconditional approval. If the lender has only "conditional" FHA approval, and is in the Pre-Closing Review phase, then the lender must submit the loan to FHA for approval prior to closing the loan.

2. Overview of the Mortgage Loan Application Process

a. Loan Application and Endorsement Process Overview

The table below describes the stages of the mortgage loan application and endorsement process.

Stage	Description
1	A borrower contacts a lender regarding a mortgage loan, and the lender determines if the loan would be eligible for FHA insurance.
2	The borrower, along with the lender's representative, completes the loan application. The loan officer collects all supporting documentation from the borrower and submits the application and documentation to the lender.
3	The lender applies for, and is assigned, an FHA case number through the FHA Connection.
4	The lender • assigns an appraiser through the FHA Connection to perform a property appraisal to determine the value of the property that is to be security for the mortgage loan, and • completes the appraisal logging in the FHA Connection.
5	The lender instructs their underwriter to perform the mortgage credit analysis to determine the borrower's ability and willingness to repay the mortgage debt, and enters the borrower income/credit information into FHA Connection.
6	The underwriter makes the underwriting decision. If the loan is • approved, the process continues with Stage 7, or • rejected the borrower is notified, and this completes the process.
7	Once the loan is approved, the lender closes the loan with the borrower.
8	After the loan is closed, the lender initiates the loan endorsement process. **Lenders not participating in Lender Insurance Program (LIP)** • complete the Insurance Application function in FHA Connection • submit the case binder to the appropriate HOC for endorsement review • submit the case binder to the HOC in hard copy form. **Lenders participating in LIP** • insure the loan through FHA Connection, and • submit the case binder in either electronic format (eCB) or in hard copy form.

9	Upon receipt of the case binder, the HOC
	
	• logs the closing package into the FHA Connection
	• performs a pre-endorsement review, and
	• issues either the
	  ■ Mortgage Insurance Certificate (MIC), or
	  ■ Non-Endorsement Notice/Notice of Rejection (NOR).

10	The HOC completes insurance endorsement processing using the logging and endorsement functions in the FHA Connection. **Result:** Once the loan is endorsed, FHA Connection generates an MIC for the lender to download from the FHA Connection.
11	To ensure that mortgage lenders understand and comply with FHA requirements, selected case binders are chosen for a post-endorsement technical review (PETR) by the HOC.

3. Restrictions on the Use of Non FHA-Approved Mortgage Brokers

a. FHA Policy Requiring the Use of an FHA Approved Lender or Broker for Loan Origination

FHA loan origination services must be performed by either a
- FHA-approved lender, or
- FHA-approved mortgage broker (loan correspondent).

An FHA-approved loan correspondent may be compensated for the actual loan origination services it performs either directly by the consumer or indirectly by the FHA-approved lender without being in violation of either the Real Estate Settlement Procedures Act (RESPA) statute and regulations or FHA regulations.

Note: While FHA regulations permit a borrower to engage a broker who is not FHA-approved to assist him/her in obtaining mortgage financing, the loan origination services may not be performed by that broker and the FHA-approved lender may not compensate the broker for such services.

b. RESPA Prohibition of Duplicative Fees

Under no circumstances may a borrower be charged a fee that is not commensurate with the amount normally charged for similar services.

RESPA prohibits the payment of duplicative fees. The payment to an unapproved broker for duplicated services amounts to an unearned fee in violation of Section 8(b) of RESPA. Further, this payment may also act as a disguised referral fee for steering the borrower to the FHA-approved lender or loan correspondent, which is in violation of section 8(a) of RESPA.

c. Specific Loan Origination Functions and Services That Must Be Provided by an FHA Approved Lender

FHA requires that the following particular origination functions and services be performed by an FHA-approved lender or loan correspondent:
- taking information from the borrower and filling out the loan application
- collecting financial information (tax returns, bank statements) and other related documents that are part of the application process
- initiating/ordering Verifications of Employment and Deposit
- initiating/ordering request for mortgage and other loan verifications
- initiating/ordering appraisals
- initiating/ordering inspections or engineering reports
- providing disclosures (truth in lending, good faith estimate and others) to the borrower(s)
- maintaining regular contact with the borrower, real estate professional, and lender between loan application and closing to apprise them of the status of the application and gather any additional information needed
- ordering legal documents, and
- determining whether the property is in a flood zone or ordering such service.

d. Services That May Be Provided by a Non FHA Approved Broker

Services that are considered counseling in nature (such as educating prospective borrowers in the home buying and financing process, advising the borrower about different types of loan products available, and demonstrating how closing costs and monthly payment could vary under each product), may be performed by a non FHA-approved broker so long as the services provided constitute meaningful counseling, and not steering.

Under RESPA, when "counseling type" services are performed, HUD also looks at whether:

- counseling gave the borrower the opportunity to consider products from at least three different lenders

- the entity performing the counseling would receive the same compensation regardless of which lender's product were ultimately selected, and

- any payment made for the "counseling type" services is reasonably related to the services performed.

> **Note:** In these instances, the fee charged must be paid from the mortgagor's own available assets and must be disclosed on the HUD-1 at closing, and a copy of the contract for these services must be included in the loan file submitted for insurance endorsement.

4. FHA Connection

I. Overview of the FHA Connection

a. Description of FHA Connection

The FHA Connection is an interactive portal on the Internet that provides approved FHA lenders real-time access to several FHA systems, including FHA's Computerized Homes Underwriting Management System (CHUMS)

b. Requirement That DE Lenders Use FHA Connection

Direct Endorsement (DE) lenders must use FHA Connection to electronically
- process case number assignments, inspector assignments, appraisal information, and case cancellations (until the process is updated), and
- receive
    - insurance, and
    - loan data.

Note: Home Ownership Centers (HOCs) will not accept telephone or mail requests for case numbers, case status, or other actions that can be performed by the lender through the FHA Connection.

c. FHA Connection Functionality

The FHA Connection provides lenders with the ability to perform the following transactions electronically:
- request
    - FHA case number assignments
    - case queries
    - insurance
    - loan data
    - (CAIVRS) authorizations
    - HECM insurance
    - appraiser assignments
    - refinance authorizations
    - inspector assignments
    - case cancellations
    - Reports, and

- transfer cases to other lenders or sponsors

- query approval lists

- create
    - Institutional Master File (IMF) sponsor relationships, and
    - Authorized agents for Title II

- register
    - underwriters, and
    - automated underwriting systems

- change IMF addresses

- inquiry IMF addresses, and

- add Title I and Title II branches.

d. Help Screen Information

A Help icon is located on the upper right hand corner of each FHA Connection screen to assist the user. The Help window describes the system:
- functions
- data entry fields
- valid data entries, and
- information that is returned to the user upon performing various functions.

Note: The Help screens should be consulted prior to calling FHA for help with the data entry fields.

e. FHA Connection Error Messages

FHA Connection users receive immediate feedback, in the form of an electronic error message, on reasons for possible non-insurance. Lenders must correct any errors before cases are submitted for insurance.

f. Requirement to Enter Appraisal Information Into FHA Connection

For all cases, including Home Equity Conversion Mortgages (HECMs)
- the appraiser must send his/her appraisal and one copy to the lender (the appraiser should not mail the appraisal to the HOC), and
- the lender is required to enter the appraisal information into the FHA Connection prior to receiving insurance

When mailing the HUD case binder to the HOC, the DE lender must include the original appraisal and copy provided by the appraiser.

Note: Lenders originating HECM loans enter the appraisal information into FHA Connection in order for the system to calculate the mortgage insurance premium (MIP).

g. FHAC B2G

The FHA Connection Business-to-Government (FHAC B2G) specification allows lenders to transmit data directly from their own internal loan processing systems to FHA without rekeying data into the FHA Connection or functional equivalent. B2G reduces the data entry burden for lenders and allows for efficient transmission of large volumes of data to FHA.

II. Accessing FHA Connection

a. Where to Access FHA Connection

The FHA Connection is accessed on the Internet
  • from the HUD Web site at www.hud.gov

b. User ID Requirement and Types of IDs

A user ID is necessary to sign onto the FHA Connection portal. The two types of user IDs that are issued are the:
  • Application Coordinator ID, and
  • Standard ID

Each lender must designate, at the corporate level, an Application Coordinator prior to requesting standard IDs.

Note: A maximum of two Application Coordinator IDs may be issued per lender at the corporate level.

c. Process for Obtaining User IDs

The table below describes the stages in the process for obtaining Application Coordinator and standard user Ids.

Stage	Description
1	The lender designates an Application Coordinator (or a maximum of two Coordinators).
2	The Application Coordinator obtains an ID by completing the FHA Application Coordinator Registration Form on the FHA Connections Web site with the following information: • name • Social Security number (SSN) • lender ID • e-mail address • mother's maiden name • desired password, and • the system name for which they are applying for the ID.
3	After successfully completing the form: • the system generates a user ID which is mailed to the lender President/CEO, and • the President/CEO forwards the ID upon receipt to the Application Coordinator. **Note:** If the President/CEO feels that the applicant should not receive this ID, he/she may contact the Help Line to have the ID terminated.
4	Once the Application Coordinator has his/her ID, other lender employees may request standard IDs for themselves by: • completing the FHA Connection ID Registration form, indicating that they are requesting standard IDs, and providing the same information as in Stage 2.

5	After the employees successfully complete the registration: • the system generates the standard IDs, and • the Application Coordinator is able to retrieve the IDs from the system.
6	The Application Coordinator uses the FHA Connection Maintenance Screen to: • grant company employees the proper authorizations and access to the different applications (such as Case Query, Appraiser Reassignment, Insurance Processing, and so on), and • remove IDs, when necessary, from the system.

III. Requests for an FHA Case Number

a. Requesting an FHA Case Number

Lenders must request and obtain an FHA case number using the FHA Connection or its functional equivalent and the lender must also use the FHA Connection to transmit any additional FHA information on a particular property.

IV. Canceling and Reinstating Case Numbers

a. Notification of Case Number Cancellation

Lenders must fax a cancellation request, specifying the reason for cancellation, to the appropriate HOC to close outstanding files and cancel an FHA case number if:
> • an appraisal has not been completed and the borrower will not close the loan as an FHA loan
> • the FHA mortgage insurance will not be sought, or
> • the appraisal has already expired.

b. Automatic Case Number Cancellations by the System

FHA's systems (FHAC/CHUMS) automatically cancel an uninsured case number 13 months after the last action taken on the loan/case.

c. Reinstatement of Case Numbers

If a case number has been canceled, and FHA insurance will be sought, the lender must fax a request to the appropriate HOC, requesting that the case number be reinstated to an active status.

V. Transferring Case Numbers Between Lenders

a. Requirements for the Transferring Lender

Transferring lenders are expected to cooperate in the transfer of case numbers. At a borrower's request, the lender must assign the case number to the new lender using the Case Transfer function in the FHA Connection. Additionally, the transferring lender:

- is not entitled to a fee for the transfer of a streamline refinance case number, regardless of the current stage of processing for the loan

- may be entitled to any lock-in fee collected from a borrower at the time of application

- is required to provide the new lender with the appraisal, but is not required to provide any processing documents.

  Note: If processing documents are provided, the lender:

  - must negotiate the fee with the new lender, and

  - is not authorized to charge the borrower a separate fee for the transfer of the processing documents.

b. New Borrower Using an Existing Appraisal

If a case number transfer involves a new borrower using an existing appraisal, the new lender
- collects an appraisal fee from the new borrower, and
- sends the fee to the original lender, who, in turn, refunds the fee to the original borrower.

c. Case Number Transfer Involving a Rejected Loan

If the transfer involves a rejected loan, the original lender must complete the Mortgage Credit Reject function in FHA Connection prior to transferring the loan.

d. Case Number Transfer Involving a MAR

If a case number transfer involves a Form HUD 91322.1, Master Appraisal Report (MAR), the transferring lender is only entitled to a pro-rata share of the cost of the MAR.

While a lender may have provided resources to obtain the MAR in anticipation of capturing most if not all of the individual mortgage loans, it may not deny an appraisal assignment request to a borrower who wishes to use an alternative mortgage lender.

  Example: If the MAR is for 100 units at a cost of $10,000, the new lender pays the transferring lender $100.

5. Policies on Interest Rates and Related Fees

a. Establishment of the Interest Rate

Under all currently active FHA single family mortgage insurance programs, the interest rate and any discount points are negotiated between the borrower and the lender.

b. Fees for Lock Ins or Rate Locks

Lenders are permitted to charge a commitment fee to guarantee, in writing, the interest rate and discount points for a specific period of time or to limit the extent to which they may change.

The minimum time for lock ins or rate locks is 15 days. The loan may close in less than 15 days at the convenience of the borrower, and the lock in fees may still be earned. Lenders must honor all such commitments.

c. Required Borrower Disclosure

The lender must provide the borrower with HUD-92900-B, HUD Interest Rate Disclosure Statement to explain that the loan terms are negotiable.

d. Circumstances Requiring Borrower Re-qualification

A borrower must be requalified if there is any increase in either
- discount points, or
- the interest rate.

6. Mortgage Loan Application Documentation Requirements

I. General Documentation Standards

a. Signing Mortgage Loan Application Forms

Mortgage loan application forms must be signed and dated by all borrowers:
- applying for the mortgage, and
- assuming responsibility for the mortgage debt.

b. Verification Form Authorization

Instead of requiring borrowers to sign multiple verification forms, the lender may ask the borrower to sign a general authorization form giving the lender blanket authority to verify information needed to process the mortgage loan application, including:
- past and present employment records
- bank accounts, and/or other investment accounts

If the lender uses a general authorization form, he/she must attach a copy of the authorization to each verification form sent out.

c. Documentation of a Borrower's Financial Position

To get a complete picture of a borrower's financial position, the lender must ask the borrower, and document borrower responses, to questions regarding the source of funds for the transaction, and intended use of the property

Note: The lender is also responsible for verifying, and documenting verification of, the borrower's identity.

d. Using Self Adhesive Labels

Lenders may use self adhesive signature labels for laser printed verifications. Each label must
- completely and clearly indicate its use, and
- contain the Privacy Act notification

e. Signing in Blank

Lenders may not ask borrowers to sign documents in blank, or on blank sheets of paper.

II. Mortgage Loan Application Documentation Requirements

a. Who Completes the Mortgage Loan Application

All borrowers must complete the mortgage loan application and all additional FHA documents.

b. Mortgage Loan Application Name Requirements

Except for nonprofit corporations that provide assistance to low and moderate income families, all mortgage loan applications must be in one or more individual's name.

Mortgage loan applications from a corporation, partnership, sole proprietorship, or trust must:
- also provide the name of one or more individuals, and
- be analyzed on the basis of the individual and the organization.

c. Contents of the Mortgage Loan Application Package

The mortgage loan application package must contain all documentation that supports the lender's decision to approve the mortgage loan.

When standard documentation does not provide enough information to support the approval decision, the lender must provide additional, explanatory statements that are consistent with information in the application. The explanatory statements must clarify or supplement the documentation submitted by the borrower.

d. Age of the Mortgage Loan Application Documentation

At the time that the loan closes, all documents in the mortgage loan application may be up to 120 days old, or 180 days old for new construction, unless:
- a different time frame is specified in this HUD handbook or in other applicable HUD

instructions, or
- the nature of the documents is such that validity for underwriting purposes is not affected by the prescribed time frame, such as with
  - divorce decrees, or
  - tax returns.

If the age of documents exceeds the above limits, written verification of the documentation must be obtained.

e. Written Verification of the Age of Mortgage Loan Application Documents

Updated, written verification of the mortgage loan application documentation must be obtained when the documents exceed the time frames.

Verification forms, or documents used as an alternate to written verification forms, must pass directly between the lender and provider without being handled or transmitted by any third party or using any third party's equipment.

No document used to process or underwrite a loan may be handled or transmitted by or through an interested third party to the transaction.

f. VOD/VOE Authenticity

The Verification of Deposit (VOD) and Verification of Employment (VOE) may be faxed documents or printed pages from the Internet if they clearly identify the source, such as containing the names of the borrower's employer or depository/investment firm.

The lender must ascertain the authenticity of the documents by examining the information included in the document's header and footer. A printed Web page must show the:
- uniform resource locator (URL) address, and
- the date and time the document was printed.

g. Requirement to Provide HUD- 92564- CN to Borrower

Lenders are required to provide form HUD-92564-CN, "For Your Protection: Get a Home Inspection" to borrowers at first contact, be it pre-qualification, pre-approval, or initial application. In any case, the lender must provide the form to the borrower no later than initial loan application.

A copy of the form in a PDF file format is available online at http://www.hud.gov

III. Mortgage Loan Application Document Processing

a. Signing and Dating Mortgage Insurance Applications

The application for mortgage insurance must be signed and dated by the borrower(s) before underwriting the loan, due to:
- various disclosure requirements, and

• the belief that borrowers are best served when required certifications are divulged as early as possible in the loan application process.

b. Using a Signed Initial URLA and Addendum

FHA recognizes the burden on lenders and borrowers of having to resign various documents after the loan application is taken. To alleviate this burden, lenders are permitted to process and underwrite the loan after the borrower completes an initial Uniform Residential Loan Application (URLA), and initial Addendum.

If the lender asks the borrower to complete an initial Addendum based on the preliminary information obtained when he/she applies for the loan, the final loan application or Addendum does not need to be signed before underwriting.

The underwriter must condition the loan approval for the final URLA and Addendum to be signed and dated by the borrower(s) anytime before or at loan closing.

c. Who Signs the Addendum

The table below describes the signatures required on different pages of the Addendum.

Page ...	Must be signed by ...
one of the initial Addendum	the interviewer.
one of the final Addendum	anyone authorized to bind the company in its business dealing with HUD.
two of the initial Addendum	the borrower(s) in two places • Part IV the borrower(s) is providing consent for the SSA to verify their own SSN, and • Part V the borrower(s) is acknowledging the certifications.
three of the final Addendum	must be signed and dated the DE underwriter, or the mortgagee representative's for "accept" or "approved" for manually or AUS approved loans, approval of loan term with the approval date and expiration date.
four of the Addendum	the borrower at loan closing.

d. Use of a Power of Attorney for Mortgage Loan Application Execution

The initial mortgage loan application may not be executed by using a power of attorney, except in circumstances as indicated in the table below.

Note: Either the initial application or the final, if used, must contain the signatures of all borrowers.

Permissible Use of a Power of Attorney for a Loan Application	Policy Description
Military personnel	A power of attorney may be used for military personnel on overseas duty or on an unaccompanied tour. The lender should obtain the service person's signature on the application by mail or fax machine.
Incapacitated borrowers	A power of attorney may be used for incapacitated borrowers who are unable to sign the mortgage application. The lender must provide evidence that the signer has authority to purchase the property and to obligate the borrower. Acceptable evidence includes a durable power of attorney specifically designed to survive incapacity and avoid the need to court proceedings. The incapacitated individual must occupy the property to be insured, except on eligible investment property.

CHAPTER TWO

Underwriting Overview

1. General Information on the Underwriting Process

a. Purpose of Underwriting

The purpose of underwriting is to

- determine a borrower's ability and willingness to repay a mortgage debt to limit the probability of default and collection difficulties, and

- examine the property offered as security for the loan to determine if it is sufficient collateral.

b. Four C's of Credit

During the underwriting process, the four C's of credit are evaluated to determine a borrower's creditworthiness. The four C's include a borrower's

- credit history
- capacity to repay the loan
- cash assets available to close the mortgage, and
- collateral.

c. FHA General Credit Policy

The Federal Housing Administration's (FHA's) general credit policy requirements for underwriting a mortgage involve

- considering the type of income for qualifying a borrower
- analyzing the liabilities to determine creditworthiness, and
- reviewing debt-to-income ratios and compensating factors.

2. General Documentation Standards

a. Signature Requirements and Use of Power of Attorney for Application Forms

All borrowers applying for the mortgage and assuming responsibility for the mortgage debt must sign the Uniform Residential Loan Application (URLA), and all addenda.

A power of attorney may be used for closing documents, including

- page four of the URLA Addendum, and
- the final URLA, if signed at closing.

Any specific or general power of attorney must comply with state law, and allow for legal enforcement of the mortgage Note in the jurisdiction.

Note: The initial loan application may not be executed by power of attorney except for military personnel and incapacitated borrowers.

b. Borrower Authorization for Verification of Information

Rather than requiring borrowers to sign multiple verification forms, the lender may ask the borrower to sign a general authorization form that gives the lender blanket authority to verify information needed to process the mortgage loan application, such as:
- past and present employment records
- bank accounts, and
- stock holdings.

If a blanket authorization is used, the lender:
- must attach a copy of the authorization to each verification sent, and
- may use self-adhesive signature labels for laser printed verifications, but each label must
  - completely and clearly indicate its use, and
  - contain the Privacy Act notification.

c. Policy Prohibiting Documents Signed in Blank

Lenders may not have borrowers sign
- documents in blank
- incomplete documents, or
- on blank sheets of paper.

d. Policy Prohibiting the Use of Documents Handled by Third Parties

Lenders may not accept or use documents relating to the credit, employment, or income of borrowers that have been handled by, or transmitted from or through the equipment of, interested third parties, such as real estate agents, builders, or sellers.

e. Verification of Employment and Asset Information Sent Via Fax or Internet

Income/employment or asset documents sent to the lender by fax must clearly identify the:
- employer or depository/investment firm's name and source of information, and
- name and telephone number of the individual at the employer or financial institution responsible for verifying the accuracy of the data.

The lender is accountable for determining the authenticity of faxed documents by examining the information included at the top or banner portion of the fax.

Likewise, income/employment or asset documentation from an Internet web site must clearly identify the employer or depository/investment firm's name and source of information. Documentation from an Internet website for depository accounts must provide the same information as a standard original statement, including account holder, account number, detailed transaction history and account balance.

Portions of the printouts downloaded from the Web pages must be examined for authenticity. Printed Web pages must:
- be placed in the case binder
- show the uniform resource locator (URL) address, and the date and time the documents were printed, and
- be derived from a web site that has been verified by the lender to have existed.

f. Requirement That All Transactions Are Scored Through TOTAL Mortgage Scorecard

TOTAL (Technology Open To Approved Lenders) Mortgage Scorecard has proven to be a successful tool for lenders to more efficiently determine borrower creditworthiness. Based on FHA's positive experience with TOTAL, the agency requires all transactions to be scored through TOTAL Mortgage Scorecard except streamline refinance transactions and transactions involving borrowers without a credit score.

3. Required Documents for Mortgage Credit Analysis

a. General Mortgage Credit Analysis Documents

The documents listed in the table below are the general documents required for mortgage credit analysis. **Note:** This is not a complete listing. Additional documentation may be required.

Loan Application

- URLA signed and dated by all borrowers and the lender, and
- Form HUD-92900-A, Addendum to the URLA

Loan Underwriting and Transmittal Summary

HUD-92900-LT, FHA Loan Underwriting and Transmittal Summary, for purchases and refinances.

Credit Report

The lender must obtain a credit report on all borrowers who will be obligated on the mortgage note, except in cases involving certain streamline refinance transactions.

Sales Contract

The lender must obtain the sales contract and any amendments or other agreements and certifications.

Real Estate Certification

If not contained within the purchase agreement, the lender must provide the real estate certification, signed by the:
- buyer
- seller, and
- selling real estate agent or broker.

Amendatory Clause

The lender must provide the amendatory clause, signed by the borrower and seller, if it is not contained in the purchase agreement.

Verification of Rent or Payment History on Past/Previous Mortgages

This document must be in the form of:
- direct written verification from the landlord or mortgage servicer
- information shown on the credit report, or
- the most recent 12 months of cancelled checks or receipts for payment of the rent/mortgage.

Explanatory Statement

The lender must include, in the case binder, any explanatory statements or additional documentation necessary to make a sound underwriting decision.

b. Evidence of Social Security Number

All individuals, including United States (U.S.) citizens, must have a valid Social Security number (SSN) and must provide evidence of that SSN to the lender.

The lender is responsible for:
- documenting an SSN for each borrower, co-borrower, and cosigner on the mortgage
- validating each SSN either through

- entering the borrower's name, date of birth and SSN in the borrower/address validation screen through the FHA Connection (FHAC) or its functional equivalent

- examination of the borrower's pay stubs, W-2, valid tax returns direct from the Internal Revenue Service (IRS), or other documentation acceptable to FHA, or

- use of a service provider, including those with direct access to the Social Security Administration (SSA), and

- resolving, if necessary, any inconsistencies or multiple SSNs for individual borrowers that are revealed during loan processing and underwriting.

Note: These requirements apply to purchase money loans and all refinances, including streamline refinances.

c. Verification of Deposit

The lender must obtain a written Verification of Deposit (VOD) and the borrower's most recent statements for all asset accounts to be used in qualifying.

"Most recent" means at the time the loan application is made. If the document is not more than **120 days old** when the loan closes (**180 days old** on new construction), it does not have to be updated.

Alternative Documentation

As an alternative to obtaining a written VOD, the lender may obtain from the borrower original asset statements covering the most recent three-month period. Provided that the asset statement shows the previous month's balance, this requirement is met by obtaining the two most recent, consecutive statements.

TOTAL Scorecard Accept Recommendation

If a written VOD is not obtained, then obtain a statement showing the previous month's ending balance for the most recent month. If the previous month's balance is not shown, obtain statement(s) for the most recent two months to verify that there are sufficient funds to close.

d. Evidence of Employment

The lender must obtain a Verification of Employment (VOE), and the borrower's most recent pay stub.

"Most recent" refers to the most recent pay stub at the time the loan application is made. If the document is not more than 120 days old when the loan closes (180 days old on new construction), it does not have to be updated.

e. Alternative VOE Documentation

As an alternative to obtaining a written VOE, the lender may obtain the borrower's:

- original pay stub(s) covering the most recent 30-day period, and
- the original IRS W-2 forms from the previous two years. (Note: Any copy of the IRS W-2 not submitted with the borrower's tax return is considered an "original." The original may be photocopied and returned to the borrower.)

The lender must also:

- verify by telephone all current employers
- include in the loan file a certification stating that original documents were examined and the name, title, and telephone number of the person with whom employment was verified
- sign and date the verification, and
- for all loans processed in this manner, obtain a signed copy of IRS 4506, Request for Copy of Tax Form, Form IRS 8821, or a document that is appropriate for obtaining tax returns directly from the IRS.

Notes:
- The lender may also use an electronic retrieval service for obtaining W-2 and tax return information.
- Standard employment documentation must be used if
  - the employer will not provide telephone confirmation of employment, or
  - the W-2(s) and/or pay stub(s) indicates inconsistencies (for example, Federal Insurance Contributions Act (FICA) payments not reflecting earnings).

f. Federal Income Tax Returns

The lender must obtain:

- Federal income tax returns for the most recent two years, both individual and business, including all applicable schedules, for self-employed borrowers, and
- individual Federal tax returns for commissioned individuals.

The lender must obtain signed forms IRS 4506, IRS 8821, or whatever form or electronic retrieval service is appropriate for obtaining tax returns directly from the IRS for any loan for which the borrower's tax returns are required.

g. Appraisal Documentation

The lender must obtain:

• Fannie Mae Form 1004MC, Market Conditions Addendum to the Appraisal Report, for all appraisals of properties that are to be security for FHA-insured mortgages performed on or after April 1, 2009, and

• one of the following Fannie Mae forms, as appropriate, and any attachments and exhibits, completed and dated by the appraiser:

■ Fannie Mae Form 1004, Uniform Residential Appraisal Report - required to report an appraisal of a one-unit property, or a one-unit property with an accessory unit

■ Fannie Mae Form 1004C, Manufactured Home Appraisal Report - required to report an appraisal of a one-unit manufactured home

■ Fannie Mae Form 1073, Individual Condominium Unit Appraisal Report - required to report an appraisal of a unit in a condominium project, or a condominium unit in a planned unit development (PUD), or

■ Fannie Mae Form 1025, Small Residential Income Property Appraisal Report - required to report an appraisal of a two- to four-unit property.

Exception: This requirement does not apply to streamline refinance transactions made without an appraisal.

4. General Information on Traditional & Non-Traditional Credit Reports

a. Required Credit Report Information

Credit reports submitted with each loan application must contain all credit information available in the accessed repositories. Additionally, for each borrower responsible for the mortgage debt, the report must contain all of the information available in the credit repositories pertaining to:
• credit
• residence history, and
• public records information.

Note: One report is required for each borrower. A joint report can be obtained for a married couple.

b. Types of Traditional Credit Reports

The two types of traditional credit reports are the:
• "three repository merged" credit report, also known as a "tri-merged" credit report (TRMCR), and
• Residential Mortgage Credit Report (RMCR).

The minimum credit report required by FHA is the TRMCR. When required, an RMCR from an independent consumer-reporting agency may also be used.

Note: An RMCR is generally required when a borrower disputes information on the TRMCR.

c. Use of Non- Traditional Credit Reports

A Non-Traditional Mortgage Credit Report (NTMCR) is:

> • designed to access the credit history of a borrower without the types of trade references normally appearing on a traditional credit report, and
> • used either as a
>> ▪ substitute for a TRMCR or an RMCR, or
>> ▪ supplement to a traditional credit report that has an insufficient number of trade items reported.

Note: A NTMCR may not be used to:

> • enhance the credit history of a borrower with a poor payment record
> • manufacture a credit report for a borrower without verifiable credit history, or
> • offset derogatory references on the borrower's traditional credit, such as collections and judgments.

d. Developing Credit Information

A lender must develop credit information separately for any open debt listed on the loan application but not referenced in the credit report.

Accounts listed as "rate by mail only" or "need written authorization" require separate written notification for traditional credit reports.

e. Credit Report Retention and Discrepancy Reconciliation

Lenders must:
> • retain all copies of all credit reports
> • document in writing an analysis of the reasons for any discrepancies between the credit reports, and
> • reconcile inconsistencies if he/she receives any information that is not consistent with information on the credit report.

5. Three Repository Merged Credit Report (TRMCR)

a. Methods of TRMCR Submission

When the lender submits the TRMCR, it must:

- be the original, and
- either be
  - sent electronically, and printed on the lender's printer, or
  - delivered by the credit-reporting agency.

b. Required TRMCR Format

The TRMCR must be in an easy-to-read and understandable format, and should not require code translations.

Whiteouts, erasures, or alterations are not permitted.

c. Required Demographic Information

The TRMCR must include:
- the name of the company ordering the report
- the name, address, and telephone number of the consumer-reporting agency
- each borrower's name and SSN, and
- for each account listed, the primary repository from which the particular information was pulled.

d. Required TRMCR Borrower Credit- Related Information

The TRMCR must include:

- all inquiries made within the last 90 days

- all credit and legal information not considered obsolete under the Fair Credit Reporting Act (FCRA), including information for the last seven years regarding
  - bankruptcies
  - law suits
  - tax liens
  - judgments
  - foreclosures

- for each borrower debt listed, the
  - date the acct was opened
  - required payment
  - payment history
  - high credit amount
  - unpaid balance, and

  - A corrected credit report must supplement the TRMCR if the report does not verify legal actions such as bankruptcies, judgments, lawsuits, foreclosures, and tax liens.

■ For any open debt listed on the loan application, but not referenced on the TRMCR, the lender must develop credit information separately.

6. Residential Mortgage Credit Report (RMCR)

a. When an RMCR Is Required

An RMCR is required when the:

- borrower(s) disputes the ownership of accounts on the TRMCR
- borrower(s) claims that collections, judgments, or liens listed as open are paid and supporting documentation supporting the claim is unavailable
- borrower claims that certain debts on the TRMCR have different balances and/or payments and current statements less than 30 days old confirming the claim are unavailable, or
- lender's underwriter determines that it is more prudent to use an RMCR in lieu of the TRMCR to underwrite the loan.

b. Required RMCR Information

RMCRs must access at least two named repositories and meet all the requirements for the TRMCR. In addition, the RMCR must:
- provide a detailed account of the borrower's employment history
- verify each borrower's current employment and income, if obtainable
- contain a statement attesting to the certification of employment for each borrower and the date verified, and
- include a check with the creditor within 90 days of the credit report for each borrower's account with a balance.

Note: If the certification of employment is not obtained through an interview with the borrower(s) employer, the credit-reporting agency must state the reason for not completing this interview.

7. Non-Traditional Credit Report (NTMCR) Requirements

a. FHA Preference for Verification of Nontraditional Credit References

FHA prefers that all nontraditional credit references be verified by a credit bureau and reported back to the lender as a nontraditional mortgage credit report (NTMCR) in the same manner as traditional credit references.

Note: Only if an NTMCR is impractical or such a service is unavailable may a lender choose to obtain independent verification of trade references.

b. Purpose of NTMCRs

A NTMCR is designed to assess the credit history of a borrower without the types of trade references normally appearing on a traditional credit report. A NTMCR can be used as a
- substitute for a TRMCR or an RMCR for a borrower without a credit history with traditional credit grantors, or
- supplement to a traditional credit report having an insufficient number of trade items reported.

c. Format for Credit References on an NTMCR

Trade references appearing on an NTMCR should be formatted in a similar fashion to traditional references, including the:
- creditor's name
- date of opening
- high credit
- current status of the account
- required payment
- unpaid balance, and
- a payment history in the delinquency categories (for example, 0x30, 0x60, and so on).

Note: The report should not include subjective statements such as "satisfactory" or "acceptable."

d. When Use of an NTMCR Is Not Permitted

A NTMCR cannot be used to

- enhance the credit history of a borrower with a poor payment record
- manufacture a credit report for a borrower without a verifiable credit history, or
- offset derogatory references found in the borrower's traditional credit report, such as collections and judgments.

e. Use of an NTMCR When There Is Insufficient Credit Report Information

Lenders may use an NTMCR developed by a credit-reporting agency that documents all non-traditional credit references when the information in the standard credit report is not sufficient for the lender to make a prudent underwriting decision.

If an NTMCR is not available, the lender must develop his/her own non-traditional credit history consistent with traditional credit report requirements.

f. Guidelines for Determining That a Borrower Has Sufficient Credit References

In order to determine that a borrower has sufficient credit references to be able to evaluate bill paying habits, the credit history must:

- include three credit references, including at least one from Group I (below), and

• exhaust all Group I references prior to considering Group II for eligibility purposes (as Group I is considered more indicative of a borrower's future housing payment performance).

The table below lists the Group I and Group II categories of credit references that can be used for determining if a borrower has a sufficient credit history.

GROUP NUMBER	TYPES OF CREDIT REFERENCES
Group I	• Rental housing payments (subject to independent verification if the borrower is a renter), • Utility company reference (if not included in the rental housing payment), including 　■ gas 　■ electricity 　■ water 　■ land-line home telephone service, and 　■ cable TV. Note: If the borrower is renting from a family member, request independent documents to prove regularity of payments, such as cancelled checks.
Group II	• Insurance premiums (for example, medical, auto, life, renter's insurance (not payroll deducted) • payment to child care providers - made to a business providing such services • school tuition • retail stores - department, furniture, appliance stores, specialty stores • rent to own - (for example, furniture, appliances) • payment of that part of medical bills not covered by insurance • Internet/cell phone services • a documented 12 month history of saving by regular deposits (at least quarterly/non-payroll deducted/no NSF checks reflected), resulting in an increasing balance to the account • automobile leases, or • a personal loan from an individual with repayment terms in writing and supported by cancelled checks to document the payments.

8. Evaluating Non-Traditional Credit and Insufficient Credit

a. Evaluating Borrowers With Insufficient Credit

When evaluating borrowers with no credit references, or otherwise having only Group II references, a satisfactory credit history, at least 12 months in duration, must include:

• no more than one 30-day delinquency on payments due to any Group II reference, and
• no collection accounts/court records reporting (other than medical) filed within the past 12 months.

b. Underwriting Guidance for Borrowers With Insufficient Credit

In order to enhance the likelihood of homeownership sustainability for borrowers with insufficient credit histories, the underwriting guidance below is provided:

• Qualifying ratios are to be computed only on those occupying the property and obligated on the loan, and may not exceed 31 percent for the payment-to-income ratio and 43 percent for the total debt-to-income ratio. Compensating factors are not applicable for borrowers with insufficient credit references.

• Borrowers should have two months of cash reserves following mortgage loan settlement from their own funds (no cash gifts from any source should be counted in the cash reserves for borrowers in this category).

CHAPTER THREE

Maximum Mortgage Amounts AND
Cash Investment Requirements on Purchase Transactions

1. Maximum Mortgage Amounts on Purchases

a. Maximum Insurable Mortgage

The maximum insurable mortgage is the lesser of the:
- statutory loan limit for the area (typically a county, or metropolitan statistical area (MSA), or
- applicable loan-to-value (LTV) limit, applied to the lesser of:
  - the sales price, or
  - the appraised value.

b. Up- Front Mortgage Insurance Payments

Most Federal Housing Administration (FHA) mortgages require the payment of an up-front mortgage insurance premium (UFMIP). The statutory loan amounts and LTV limits discussed in this handbook do not include the UFMIP.

c. Statutory Loan Limits

Statutory loan amount limits vary by program and the number of family units within the dwelling.

d. LTV Limits

The determination of the maximum LTV percentage available to the borrower is influenced by:
- the particular mortgage insurance program
- the property type (for example, new or existing construction), and
- various transactions that affect the maximum mortgage calculation

Once determined, the LTV percentage is then applied to the lesser of the sales price or the appraised value in order to determine the maximum insurable mortgage.

I. Calculating Maximum Mortgage Amounts on Purchases

a. Maximum Mortgage Amount Calculation

The maximum mortgage amount that FHA will insure is calculated by multiplying the appropriate LTV factor by the lesser of the property's:

- sales price, subject to certain required adjustments, or
- appraised value.

In order for FHA to insure this maximum loan amount, the borrower must make a required investment of at least 3.5 percent of the lesser of the appraised value of the property or the sales price.

b. Maximum LTV for Proposed/ Existing Construction

For purchase transactions, the maximum LTV is 96.5 percent (that is, the reciprocal of the 3.5 percent required investment).

c. Borrower Required Investment on a Purchase Transaction

The borrower must make a required investment at least equal to 3.5 percent of the lesser of the appraised value of the property or the sales price.

d. Policy on Closing Costs

Closing costs (non-recurring closing costs, pre-paid expenses, and discount points) may not be used to help meet the minimum 3.5 percent required investment.

e. Credit Card Payment for the Appraisal/ Credit Report

The borrower may use a credit card to pay for the appraisal and credit report. These costs cannot be considered to help meet the required investment.

II. Interested Third Party Contributions

a. Definition: Third Party Contribution

A Third Party Contribution is a payment by a seller and/or an interested third party, or a combination of parties toward the borrower's costs to close.

b. Interested Third Party Contribution Amounts

The seller and/or third party may contribute up to six percent of the lesser of the property's sales price or the appraised value toward the buyer's closing costs, prepaid expenses, discount points and other financing concessions.

The six percent limit also includes

- third party payment for permanent and temporary interest rate buydowns, and other payment supplements
- payments of mortgage interest for fixed rate mortgages
- mortgage payment protection insurance, and
- payment of UFMIP.

Note: Contributions exceeding six percent are considered inducements to purchase.

c. Charges Not Considered Interested Third Party Contributions

Payment of real estate commissions or fees, typically paid by the seller under local or state law or local custom, is not considered an interested third party contribution.

d. Treatment of Amounts Exceeding Contribution Limit

Each dollar that exceeds the 6 percent limit must be subtracted from the property's sales price before applying the appropriate LTV factor.

III. Inducements to Purchase

a. Payments Considered Inducements to Purchase

Certain expenses, paid by the seller and/or an interested third party, on behalf of the borrower, are considered "inducements to purchase" and result in a dollar-for-dollar reduction to the lesser of the sales price or appraised value of the property before applying the appropriate LTV factor. These expenses include:
- contributions exceeding 6 percent of the sales price
- contributions exceeding the actual cost of prepaid expenses, discount points, and other financing concessions
- decorating allowances
- repair allowances
- moving costs, and
- other costs as determined by the appropriate HOC.

b. Personal Property Inducements

Personal property given by a seller and/or an interested third party to consummate the sale of a property results in a reduction in the mortgage amount. The value of the item(s) must be deducted from the lesser of the sales price or appraised value of the property before applying the LTV factor.

Depending on local custom or law, certain items may be considered as part of the real estate transaction with no adjustment to the sales price or appraised value. The table below describes how to determine if personal property affects the sales price or appraised value.

If the personal property item is a ...	Then ...
• car • boat • riding lawn mower • furniture, or • television	deduct the value of the item(s) from the sales price and appraised value before applying the LTV factor.
• range • refrigerator • dishwasher • washer • dryer • carpeting • window treatment, or • other items determined appropriate by the (HOC)	the HOC determines if the items are considered customary and affect the value of the property before applying the LTV factor. **Exception:** Replacement of existing equipment or other realty items by the seller before closing, such as carpeting or air conditioners, does not require a value adjustment provided that a cash allowance is not given to the borrower.

c. Conditions for Subtracting Sales Commissions

Sales commissions paid by an interested third party on a borrower's present residence can be considered inducements to purchase, and should be subtracted from the sales price before applying the LTV factor.

The table below describes the conditions under which a sales commission is subtracted from the sales price before applying the LTV factor.

If ...	Then ...
• the seller and/or interested third party agrees to pay any portion of the borrower's sales commission on the sale of the borrower's present residence	• treat the amount paid by the interested third party as an inducement to purchase, and • subtract dollar-for-dollar the amount paid by the seller or builder from the lesser of the sales price or appraised value before applying the LTV factor.
• a borrower is not paying a real estate commission on the sale of his/her present home • the same real estate broker or agent is involved in both transactions, and • the seller of the property being purchased by the buyer is paying a real estate commission that exceeds what is typical for the area	• treat the amount of commission paid by the seller that exceeds what is typical for the area as an inducement to purchase, and • deduct that amount, dollar-for-dollar, from the lesser of the sales price or appraised value before applying the LTV factor.

IV. Additions to the Mortgage Amount for Repair and Improvement

a. Policy on Adding Repair and Improvement Costs to Sales Price

Repairs and improvements may be added to the sales price before calculating the mortgage amount when:
- the repairs and improvements are
  - required by the appraiser as essential for property eligibility, and
  - paid by the borrower, and

- the sales contract or addendum identifies the borrower as responsible for
  - payment, and
  - completion of the repairs.

Important: Only repairs and improvements required by the appraiser may be included.

b. Repair and Improvement Amount That Can Be Added to Sales Price

The repair and improvement amount that may be added to the sales price before calculating the maximum mortgage amount is the lowest of the:

- amount that the value of the property exceeds the sales price
- the appraiser's estimate of repairs and improvements, or
- the amount of the contractor's bid, if available.

c. Repair and Improvement Exclusions

Repairs and improvements completed by the borrower before the appraisal are not eligible to be included when calculating the maximum mortgage. This amount becomes part of the borrower's required cash investment.

d. Energy- Related Weatherization Items

The mortgage amount may be increased if the cost of energy-related weatherization items paid by the borrower is added to the property. Examples of energy-related weatherization items include:

- thermostats
- insulation
- weather stripping and caulking
- storm windows and doors

These items may be added to both the sales price and the appraised value before determining the maximum mortgage amount.

Note: A contractor's statement of the cost of work completed, or a buyer's estimate of the cost of materials must be submitted.

e. Calculating the Energy- Related Mortgage Amount

The energy-related amount that can be added when calculating the maximum mortgage amount is either:

- $2,000 without a separate value determination
- up to $3,500, if supported by a value determination by an approved FHA roster appraiser or Direct Endorsement (DE) Underwriter, or
- more than $3,500
  - subject to a value determination by an approved FHA roster appraiser or DE Underwriter, and
  - with a separate on-site inspection made by a FHA-approved fee inspector or DE staff appraiser.

f. When Energy Related Items Cannot Be Completed Prior to Closing

If repairs and energy-related items cannot be completed before loan closing due to weather-related delays, the lender must establish an escrow account to ensure all required repairs are eventually completed.

g. Adding Solar Energy System Costs

The cost of solar energy systems may be added directly to the mortgage amount before adding the UFMIP, and after applying the LTV factor limits.

The amount added is limited to the lesser of the solar energy system's
- replacement cost, or
- effect on the property's market value.

The statutory mortgage limit for the area also may be exceeded by 20 percent to accommodate the cost of the system.

Note: Active and passive solar systems, as well as wind-driven systems are acceptable.

i. Energy Efficient Mortgage Calculation

If the energy efficient improvements are "cost effective" as determined by the lender based upon the report from the HERS or energy consultant, 100 percent of the cost of the energy efficient improvements (subject to certain limits) may be added to the mortgage amount.

2. Transactions Affecting Maximum Mortgage Calculations

I. General Information on Transactions Affecting Maximum Mortgage Calculations

a. Types of Transactions

Certain types of loan transactions affect the amount of financing available to a borrower, and determine how to calculate the maximum mortgage amount. The types of transactions include:

- identity-of-interest

- properties with non-occupying co-borrowers

- three- and four-unit properties

- properties where a house will be constructed by a borrower
  - on his/her land, and/or
  - as a licensed general contractor

- payoffs of land contracts, and

- transactions involving properties
  - under construction, or
  - less than a year old.

II. Identity of Interest Transactions

a. Definition: Identity of Interest Transaction

An identity of interest transaction is a sales transaction between parties with family or business relationships.

b. Maximum LTV Factor on Identity of Interest Transactions

The maximum LTV factor for identity of interest transactions on principal residences is restricted to 85 percent.

c. Exceptions to the Maximum LTV Factor for Identity of Interest LTV Transactions

Maximum financing above the 85 percent is permitted under certain circumstances. The table below describes circumstances in which financing above the 85 percent is permitted.

Exception	Description
Family Member Purchase	A family member purchases another family member's home as a principal residence. If the property is sold from one family member to another and is the seller's investment property, the maximum mortgage is the lesser of •85 percent of the appraised value, or •the appropriate LTV factor percentage applied to the sales price, plus or minus required adjustments. *Note:* The 85% limit may be waived if the family member has been a tenant in the property for at least six months immediately predating the sales contract. A lease or other written evidence must be submitted to verify occupancy.
Builder's Employee Purchase	An employee of a builder purchases one of the builder's new homes or models as a principal residence.
Tenant Purchase	A current tenant, including a family member tenant, purchases the property where he/she has rented for at least six months immediately predating the sales contract. *Note:* A lease or other written evidence to verify occupancy is required. The maximum mortgage calculation is not affected by a sales transaction between a tenant and a landlord with no identity of interest relationship.
Corporate Transfer	**A corporation** •transfers an employee to another location •purchases the employee's home, and •sells the home to another employee.

III. Non Occupying Borrowers

a. Definition: Non Occupying Borrower Transaction

A non occupying borrower transaction is a transaction involving two or more borrowers where one or more borrower(s) will not occupy the property as his/her primary residence.

b. Maximum LTV Factor for Non Occupying Borrower Transaction

When there are two or more borrowers, but one or more will not occupy the property as a principal residence, the maximum mortgage is limited to a 75 percent LTV. However, maximum financing, is available for:
- borrowers related by blood, marriage, or law, such as
  - spouses
  - parent-child
  - siblings
  - stepchildren
  - aunts-uncles, and
  - nieces-nephews, or
- unrelated individuals that can document evidence of a family-type, longstanding, and substantial relationship not arising out of the loan transaction.

Note: If a parent is selling to a child, the parent cannot be the co-borrower with the child, unless the LTV is 75 percent or less.

c. Security Instrument and Note Signature Requirement

All borrowers, regardless of occupancy status, must sign the security instrument and mortgage note. **Note:** Cosigners do not execute the security instrument or take title, but they must sign the mortgage note.

d. LTV for Two to Four Unit Properties

To reduce risk exposure, mortgages with non-occupying borrowers are limited to one-unit properties if the LTV exceeds 75 percent. The non-occupying borrower arrangement to assist in financing a property may not be used to develop a portfolio of rental properties. The financial contribution by the non-occupying borrower and the number of properties owned may indicate that the family members are acting as "strawbuyers."

e. Underwriting Criteria for Non Occupying Borrowers

FHA does not require that additional underwriting criteria, such as specific qualifying ratios, be met by either non-occupying borrowers, or occupying borrowers with sufficient credit.

However, additional FHA underwriting criteria does apply to occupying borrowers with insufficient credit.

IV. Transactions Involving Three and Four Unit Properties

a. Three and Four Unit Property Mortgage Limit/Self- Sufficiency Test

The maximum mortgage for three and four unit properties is limited, so that the ratio of the monthly mortgage payment, divided by the monthly net rental income does not exceed 100 percent, regardless of the occupancy status.

Form HUD 92561, Borrower's Contract with Respect to Hotel and Transient Use of Property is required at application for all multi-unit properties.

b. What Is Included in the Monthly Payment Calculation for Three and Four Unit Properties

The monthly mortgage payment calculation for three and four unit properties includes the following:
- principal
- interest
- taxes
- insurance (Principle, Interest, Taxes, and Insurance - PITI), including monthly mortgage insurance, and
- homeowner association dues computed at the note rate, if applicable

c. Net Rental Income Calculation for Three and Four Unit Properties

Net rental income for three and four unit property is calculated using the following formula:
- the appraiser's estimate of fair market rent from all units, including the unit the borrower chooses for occupancy, and
- minus the greater of the
  - appraiser's estimate for vacancies, or
  - vacancy factor used by the jurisdictional HOC.

This net rental income calculation is used to determine the maximum loan amount. Borrowers must still qualify for the mortgage based on:
- income
- credit
- cash to close, and
- projected rents received from remaining units

Projected rent may only be considered gross income for qualifying purposes. It cannot be used to offset the monthly mortgage payment.

d. Three and Four Unit Property Mortgage Reserves

For three- and four-unit properties, the borrower must have personal reserves equivalent to three months' PITI after closing on purchase transactions. Reserves cannot be derived from a gift.

V. Loan Transactions for Building on Own Land

a. Financing Limits When Building on Own Land

A borrower is eligible for maximum financing when he/she:

- acts as a licensed general contractor and is building a home on land that he/she already owns or acquires separately, and
- receives no cash from the settlement.

b. LTV Limits When Building on Own Land

When building on a borrower's own property, the appropriate LTV limits are applied to the lesser of the:
- appraised value of the proposed home and land, or
- documented cost of the property.

The documented cost of property includes the following:

- the builder's price, or sum of all subcontractor bids and materials
- cost of the land (if the land has been owned more than six months or was received as an acceptable gift, the value of the land may be used instead of its cost), and

• interest and other costs associated with any construction loan obtained by the borrower to fund construction of the property.

c. Using Equity When Building on Own Land

Equity in the land (value or cost, as appropriate, minus the amount owed) may be used for the borrower's entire cash investment. However, if the borrower receives more than $500 cash at closing, the loan is limited to 85 percent of the appraised value.

Replenishing the borrower's own cash expended during construction is not considered as "cash back," provided that the borrower can substantiate with cancelled checks and paid receipts all out-of-pocket funds used for construction.

d. Determining If the Borrower Has Made the Required Down Payment When Building on Own Land

In order to determine if a borrower has made the required 3.5 percent cash investment, or its equivalent in land equity when building on his/her own land, all such mortgage transactions must be summarized using only HUD-92900-LT, FHA Loan Underwriting and Transmittal Summary.

Lenders are reminded that they must record the sum total of the documented cost of the property, including:

- the builder's price, or the sum of all subcontractor costs, materials, etc.
- the cost of the land or, if owned for more than six months or was received as an acceptable gift, its appraised value, and
- interest and other costs associated with any construction loan obtained by the borrower to fund construction of the property.

Additionally, the calculated loan-to-value ratio (which is to be the same value used when seeking a risk clarification from FHA's TOTAL), must reflect, as it does on other purchase transactions, the lesser of:
- the sales price, or
- the appraised value.

VI. Loan Transactions for Paying Off Land Contracts

a. Financing Limit When Paying Off Land Contracts

If a borrower does not receive cash at closing, his/her new mortgage may be processed as a purchase or refinance transaction with maximum FHA-insured financing if he/she uses the loan to:
- complete payment on a land contract
- contract for deed, or
- other similar type of financing arrangement in which the borrower does not have title to the property.

b. LTV Factor When Paying Off Land Contracts

When the loan proceeds are used to pay the outstanding balance on the land contract and eligible repairs and renovations, if the property was acquired less than 12 months the LTV factor is applied to the lesser of the:
- appraised value of the land and improvements, or
- total cost to acquire the property, which includes the original purchase price, plus any documented costs the borrower incurs for rehabilitation, repairs, renovation, or weatherization, closing costs and reasonable discount points, if treated as a refinance.

c. Using Equity When Paying Off Land Contracts

Equity in the property (original sales price minus the amount owed) may be used for the borrower's entire cash investment. However, if the borrower receives more than $500 cash at closing, the loan is limited to 85 percent of the lesser of, if the property was acquired less than 12 months:

- appraised value of the land and improvements, or
- total cost to acquire the property, which includes the original purchase price, plus any documented costs the borrower incurs for rehabilitation, repairs, renovation, weatherization, closing costs and reasonable discount points, if treated as a refinance.

Replenishing the borrower's own cash expended for repairs, improvements, renovation, or weatherization is not considered as "cash back," provided that the borrower can substantiate with cancelled checks and paid receipts all out-of-pocket funds for the improvements.

VII. Transactions Involving Properties for Proposed Construction, Under Construction or Existing Construction Less Than One Year Old

a. Financing Limit

Properties that are proposed, under construction or existing construction less than one year old are limited to 90 percent financing.

The 90 percent financing for properties proposed, under construction, or existing construction less than one year old is calculated by using the lesser of the:

- appraiser's estimate of value, or
- sales price, plus or minus required adjustments for
  - seller contributions
  - inducements to purchase, and/or
  - additions to the mortgage amount.

b. Criteria for Maximum Financing

The table below describes the criteria that properties must meet to be eligible for greater than 90 percent financing, whether or not the property has been previously occupied.

One of those criteria must be evidenced in order for the borrower to be eligible for a high ratio mortgage.

Criteria	Description
Approval of Dwelling Site Plans	The dwelling's site plans and materials were approved before construction began by • the Department of Veterans Affairs (VA) • an eligible DE underwriter, i.e. Conditional Commitment issued prior to framing, or • an early start letter issued by a DE underwriter.

Local Jurisdiction Building Permit and Certificate of Occupancy	The local jurisdiction has issued both a
	
	  • building permit or equivalent prior to construction, and
	  • Certificate of Occupancy or equivalent.
	
	Note: This does not apply to condominiums or manufactured housing. These properties have special circumstances for financing approval.

Builder's Warranty	The dwelling is covered by a builder's ten-year insured warranty plan that is acceptable to HUD.

Dwelling Relocation	The dwelling
	
	  • will be moved to a new location, and
	  • is eligible for an insured mortgage at the new location based on approval of the dwelling site plan criteria listed previously in this table.

VIII. Manufactured Home Construction-Permanent Loans

a. Manufactured Home CP Loan is a Purchase Transaction

For purposes of underwriting and calculating the maximum mortgage amount, the CP loan on a newly-constructed manufactured home should be considered a purchase loan transaction, requiring a minimum 3.5% cash investment of the Total Cost or Value (including land).

To maintain consistency with FHA Connection data requirements and the Uniform Residential Loan Application, the purpose of the loan transaction should be designated as "CP."

b. Basic Criteria for Determining Maximum Mortgage Amount for Manufactured Home CP Loan

To determine the maximum insurable mortgage amount for a manufactured housing CP transaction, the lender must consider the: property status, length of ownership, and accepted formula to determine value.

The length of time the property was owned in a given property status will determine whether a transaction is considered a CP or refinance transaction. CP transactions involve manufactured homes with acceptable property status that are:

- proposed for construction

- under construction, or

- existing construction less than 12 months old.

c. Determining Property Status for a Manufactured Home

Property status refers to whether or not the property is classified or taxed as real property and whether the personal property title has been purged in compliance with state law.

d. Determining Length of Ownership for a Manufactured Home

Length of ownership refers to how long the prospective borrower has held an ownership interest in the manufactured housing unit and land.

e. Formulas for Determining Maximum Mortgage Amount on a Manufactured Home CP Loan

The accepted formula to determine total cost or itemized value refers to calculating the mortgage amount based on:

- total cost or itemized value

- maximum allowable loan-to-value (LTV) percentages, and

- existing indebtedness.

In a CP transaction, itemized value should be applied when the manufactured home unit, the land, or both have been owned for 6 months or more, and less than 12 months. If either the unit or the land has been owned for less than 6 months, the lesser of total cost or itemized value should be applied.

Evidence must be provided to certify how long the borrower has owned the land and/or manufactured unit. A contract or payoff statement for the land is required if it is currently encumbered by a lien payable by the borrower.

f. Maximum Mortgage Calculation for Manufactured Home CP Loan Based on Total Cost or Itemized Value

1. Mortgage Amount based on Total Cost or Itemized Value

a. Total Cost or Itemized Value:

Unit   _____   _____
Land   _____

OR

Combined   _____   _____
Construction

Hard Costs   _____
Soft Costs   _____   _____

Total Cost or Itemized Value Cost   _____

b. Minimum Cash Investment

Total Cost or Itemized Value from 1a
x 3.5% Required Statutory Investment   _____

c. Subtract Minimum Cash Investment from Total Cost or Itemized Value

Amount based on Total Cost or Itemized
Value (1a-1b)   _____

g. Maximum Mortgage Calculation for Manufactured Home CP Loan Based on Allowable LTV

2. Amount based on Maximum Allowable Loan-to-Value Percentages

Lesser of Total Cost or Itemized Value or Appraised Value x Applicable
Maximum Loan-to-Value Percentage: 96.5% for purchase transactions

Amount based on Maximum Allowable Loan-to-Value Percentages   _____

h. Maximum Mortgage Calculation for Manufactured Home CP Loan Based on Existing Indebtedness

3. Amount Based on Existing Indebtedness

Maximum Mortgage Calculation for Manufactured Home CP Loan Based on Existing Indebtedness

Unit	_____
Less Trade-in	(_____)
Land	_____
Construction	
Hard Costs	_____
Soft Costs	_____
Borrower Paid:	
Discount Points	_____
Prepaids	_____
Closing Costs	_____
Amount based on Existing Indebtedness	_____

i. Additional Concerns for Calculating the Maximum Mortgage Amount on Manufactured Home CP Loan

Financing on a manufactured home being constructed and installed is considered a construction loan or construction line-of-credit. Associated construction financing costs are to be itemized on a draw request or cost breakdown form. The file must include the contract or sales invoice for the manufactured home unit and the contract for the land.

The construction loan [hard] costs and construction loan financing [soft] costs must be identified. Lenders may obtain and provide information from the general contractor or another party who has knowledge of the related costs for completion of required work items.

The major installation charges require supporting documentation and separate invoices for the manufactured unit and the contractor's foundation and set-up costs. Razing and removing existing properties is considered part of the site preparation and may be included in the calculations as a component of the construction costs.

If the manufactured home dealer is the general contractor for the foundation and installation, the cost of the unit and additional charges must be itemized on an invoice. Aggregate amounts for total costs are not acceptable.

CHAPTER FOUR

Refinance Transaction Overview

1. General Information on Refinance Transactions

a. Purpose of a Refinance Transaction

A refinance transaction is used to pay off an existing real estate debt with the proceeds of a new mortgage:
- for borrower(s) with legal title, and
- on the same property.

> **Note:** The borrower is eligible to refinance the loan, as long as he/she has legal title, even if he/she was not originally on the loan.

b. Maximum Percentage of Financing

The maximum percentage of financing is governed by:

- the occupancy status of the property
- the use of the loan proceeds, and
- how and when the property was purchased.

Generally, the maximum mortgage may never exceed the statutory limit, except by the amount of any new upfront mortgage insurance premium (UFMIP). However, the maximum mortgage may exceed the statutory limit on certain specialty products.

> **Note:** Most Federal Housing Administration (FHA) mortgages require payment of an UFMIP. The statutory loan amount and loan-to-value (LTV) limits described in this handbook do not include UFMIP.

c. Types of Refinances

FHA insures several different types of refinance transactions, including:

- streamline refinances of existing FHA-insured mortgages made with and without

appraisals
- no cash out refinances (rate and term) of conventional and FHA-insured mortgages, where all proceeds are used to pay existing liens and costs associated with the transactions, and
- cash out refinances.

d. Maximum Refinancing Term

The maximum term of any refinance with an appraisal is 30 years.

The maximum term of a streamline refinance without an appraisal is limited to the lesser of

- the remaining term of the existing mortgage, plus 12 years, or
- 30 years.

e. Re-Using an Appraisal

FHA appraisals on existing properties are valid for six months. However, appraisals cannot be reused:
- during the six month validity period once the mortgage for which the appraisal was ordered has closed, or
- for a subsequent refinance, even if six months have not passed.

A new appraisal is required for each refinance transaction requiring an appraisal.

f. Refinance Authorization Numbers for FHA- to- FHA Refinances

A lender must obtain a Refinance Authorization Number from the FHA Connection, or functional equivalent, for all FHA-to-FHA refinances.

g. Maximum LTV Factors and UFMIP for Various Types of Refinance Transactions

The table below lists the maximum LTV factors and UFMIP for various types of refinance transactions.

Type of Refinance	Maximum LTV	UFMIP
Rate and Term	97.75%	1.75%
FHA-to-FHA Streamline w/Appraisal	97.75%	1.50%
FHA-to-FHA Streamline w/o Appraisal	N/A	1.50%
Cash Out Refinance	85%	1.75%

h. Skipped Payments Are Not Acceptable

Lenders are not permitted to allow borrowers to "skip" payments. The borrower must either:
- make the payment when it is due, or
- bring the monthly mortgage payment check to settlement.

When the new mortgage amount is calculated, FHA does not permit the inclusion of any mortgage payments "skipped" by the borrower in the new mortgage amount.

i. Refinance Transactions on Manufactured Homes

For a transaction involving a manufactured home to be considered a refinance, the manufactured home must:
- have acceptable property status
- be complete, and
- have been permanently erected on a site for more than one year (12 months) prior to the date of the application for mortgage insurance.

Standard maximum mortgage calculations apply.

j. Pay-Off Statements For Liens Held Against Subject Property

A lender must obtain pay-off statements for all liens which are to be satisfied from the proceeds of a refinance transaction. It is the responsibility of the lender to review and ascertain any lien against the subject property which is subject to payments, that the lien/loan/mortgage is current for the month due for streamline and cash-out refinance transactions.

2. Maximum Mortgage Amounts On No Cash Out/Cash Out Refinances

a. Maximum Mortgage Calculation

The maximum mortgage for a no cash out refinancing with an appraisal (credit qualifying) is the lesser of the:
- 97.75% LTV factor applied to appraised value of the property, or
- existing debt.

The total FHA first mortgage is limited to 100% of the appraised value, including any financed upfront mortgage insurance premium (UFMIP).

Most FHA mortgages require payment of an UFMIP. The statutory loan amounts and LTV limits described in this handbook do not include the UFMIP.

Generally, the maximum mortgage may never exceed the statutory limit, except by the amount of any new UFMIP. However, the maximum mortgage may exceed the statutory limit on certain specialty products.

Note: The borrower must comply with any appraisal requirements, including repairs, before the mortgage is eligible for insurance endorsement.

b. Calculating the Existing Debt on a No Cash Out Refinance With an Appraisal

Follow the steps in the table below to calculate the existing debt.

Note: On this type of refinance transaction, the borrower may not receive cash back in excess of $500 at closing.

Step	Action
1	Determine the amount of the existing first mortgage. The existing first mortgage must be current for the month due and • may include ▪ the interest charged by the servicing lender when the payoff will not likely be received on the first day of the month (as is typically assessed on FHA-insured mortgages), and ▪ any prepayment penalties assessed on a conventional mortgage or FHA Title I loan ▪ late charges, and ▪ escrow shortages, and • may not include delinquent interest.
2	Determine the prepaid expenses, which may include • the per diem interest to the end of the month on the new loan • hazard insurance premium deposits • monthly mortgage insurance premiums, and • any real estate tax deposits needed to establish the escrow account.
3	Add the following to the existing first mortgage amount: • any purchase money second mortgage • any junior liens over 12 months old • closing costs • prepaid expenses (even if the mortgagee refinancing the loan is the servicing lender) • borrower paid repairs required by the appraisal, and • discount points. **Note:** If the balance or any portion of an equity line of credit in excess of $1000 was advanced within the past 12 months and was for purposes other than repairs and rehabilitation of the property, that portion above and beyond $1,000 of the line of credit is not eligible for inclusion in the new mortgage.
4	Subtract any refund of UFMIP. **Result:** The resulting figure is the existing debt.

c. Subordinate Liens

Subordinate liens, including lines of credit, regardless of when taken, may remain outstanding (but subordinate to the FHA-insured mortgage), provided the FHA insured mortgage meets the eligibility criteria for mortgages with secondary financing.

d. Refinancing to Buy Out Ex-Spouse or Co-borrower Equity

When the purpose of the new loan is to refinance an existing mortgage in order to buy out an ex-spouse's or other co-borrower's equity, the specified equity to be paid is:

- considered property-related indebtedness, and
- eligible to be included in the new mortgage calculation.

The divorce decree, settlement agreement, or other bona fide equity agreement must be provided to document the equity awarded to the ex-spouse or co-borrower.

e. Mortgage Calculation for a Property Acquired Less Than One Year Before Loan Application

If the property was acquired less than one year before the loan application, and is not already FHA-insured, in addition to the calculations described previously in this topic, the original sales price of the property must also be considered in determining the maximum mortgage.

Using conclusive documentation, expenditures for repairs and rehabilitation incurred after the purchase of the property may be added to the original sales price in calculating the mortgage amount.

The maximum mortgage amount will be based off of the lesser of the:

- total cost to acquire the property, which includes the original purchase price plus any
  - documented costs incurred for rehabilitation, repairs, renovation, or weatherization
  - closing costs, and
  - reasonable discount points, or
- current appraised value, or
- total of all mortgage liens held against the subject property.

f. Short Pay Offs

To be eligible for refinancing with a short pay off, borrowers must be current on their mortgages.

FHA will insure the first mortgage where the existing note holder(s) write off the amount of the Indebtedness that cannot be refinanced into the new FHA-insured mortgage if

- there is insufficient equity in the home based on its current appraised value, and/or
- the borrower has experienced a reduction in income and does not have the capacity to repay the existing indebtedness against the property.

For instances where the existing note holders are reluctant to write down indebtedness, a new subordinate lien may be executed for the amount by which the payoff is short.

If payments on subordinate financing are required, they must be included in the qualifying ratios unless payments have been deferred for no less than 36 months. This policy applies only to no cash-out (rate and term) refinances with short pay offs.

3. Cash Out Refinance Transactions

a. Eligibility for Cash Out Refinances

Cash out refinance transactions are only permitted on owner occupied principal residences and properties owned free and clear may be refinanced as cash out transactions.

b. Ineligibility of Delinquent Borrowers for Cash Out Refinances

Borrowers who are delinquent, in arrears or have suffered any mortgage delinquencies within the most recent 12 month period under the terms and conditions of their mortgage are not eligible for cash out refinances.

c. Restriction on Addition of Non- Occupant Co-borrower for Credit Underwriting Compliance

Non-occupant co-borrowers may not be added in a cash out refinance transaction in order to meet FHA's credit underwriting guidelines for the mortgage. Any co-borrower or cosigner being added to the Note must be an occupant of the property.

d. No Delinquencies on Mortgage for Previous 12 Months to Be Eligible for a Cash Out Refinance

If a property is encumbered by a mortgage, the borrower must have made all of his/her mortgage payments on time within the month due for the previous 12 months.

e. Subordinate Liens and CLTV Ratios on Cash Out Refinances

The table below lists the policy requirements regarding subordinate financing and CLTVs.

Type of Subordinate Lien	Policy Requirement
New subordinate financing	If new subordinate financing is being offered by the lender or other permitted entity, the CLTV is limited to 85% (the FHA-insured first mortgage and any new junior liens when added together)

Existing subordinate financing	Existing subordinate financing may remain in place, but subordinate to the FHA-insured first mortgage, regardless of the total indebtedness or CTLV ratio, provided the borrower qualifies for making scheduled payments on all liens.
Modified subordinate lien	Many subordinate lien holders request modifications to the terms of the lien (typically a reduction in the amount of the lien) in exchange for remaining in a subordinate position. Modifying the subordinate lien in this manner often results in re-executing the lien at closing, which is acceptable to FHA. In this case, FHA does not consider the lien a new subordinate lien.

f. Maximum Mortgage Amount Calculation Based on Length of Ownership

The table below describes policy guidance on the maximum mortgage amount calculation for cash out refinance transactions, based on the length of ownership.

If the property has been owned by the borrower as his/her principal residence for ...	Then the mortgage ...
12 months or more preceding the date of the loan application	is eligible for the maximum amount of 85% of the appraiser's estimate of value.
less than 12 months preceding the date of the loan application	is limited to the lesser of 85% of the • appraiser's estimate of value, and • sales price of the property when acquired **Note:** The sales price does not need to be considered if the property was acquired as the result of inheritance and is, or will become, the heir's principal residence.

g. Risk on Cash Out Refinancing for Debt Consolidation

Cash out refinancing for debt consolidation represents considerable risk, especially if the borrowers have not had a corresponding increase in income. **Careful evaluation of this type of transaction is required.**

4. Maximum Mortgage Amounts on Streamline Refinances

I. General Information on Streamline Refinances

a. Purpose of a Streamline Refinance

Streamline refinances:
• are designed to lower the monthly principal and interest payments on a current FHA-insured mortgage, and
• must involve no cash back to the borrower, except for minor adjustments at closing, not to exceed $500.

Streamline refinances can be made with or without an appraisal.

II. Streamline Refinances Without an Appraisal

a. Streamline Refinancing Mortgage Limits

Generally, the streamline refinance mortgage amount may never exceed the statutory limits, except by the amount of any new UFMIP. However, the maximum mortgage may exceed the statutory limits on certain specialty products.

b. Maximum Mortgage Term for Streamline Refinances

The streamline refinance mortgage term is the lesser of 30 years, or the remaining term of the mortgage plus 12 years.

c. Maximum Insurable Mortgage Calculation for Streamline Refinances Without an Appraisal

The maximum insurable mortgage for streamline refinances without an appraisal cannot exceed the outstanding principal balance:
• minus the applicable refund of the Upfront Mortgage Insurance Premium (UFMIP),
• plus the new UFMIP that will be charged on the refinance.

Note: The outstanding principal balance may include interest charged by the servicing lender when the payoff is not received on the first day of the month, but may not include delinquent interest, late charges or escrow shortages.

d. Applicability of the Mortgage Calculation Process

The mortgage calculation process applies only to owner occupied properties. Non owner occupant properties, even if originally acquired as principal residences by the current borrowers, may only be refinanced for the outstanding principal balance.

e. Streamline Refinances For Non Owner Occupant Properties

Streamline financing by investors, or for secondary residences may only be made without an appraisal. The loan must be made solely in the business entity's name, if the residence was previously insured in the business entity's name.

The new security instruments must contain FHA's standard provision permitting acceleration of the mortgage when assumed by an investor, or as a secondary residence. However, FHA does not authorize the lender to exercise the acceleration provision if the investor assumptor is found to be creditworthy.

Although a property purchased as a principal residence, under certain circumstances as described in the security instruments, may be rented or become a secondary residence, a streamline refinance without an appraisal does not "convert" the mortgage to one eligible for assumption by an investor.

f. Policy on Subordinate Financing on Streamline Refinances Without an Appraisal

Subordinate liens, including credit lines, regardless of when taken, may remain outstanding, but must be subordinate to the FHA-insured mortgage.

If subordinate financing remains in place, the:
- maximum combined loan-to-value (CLTV) is 125 percent
- CLTV is based on the original appraised value of the property, and
- maximum CLTV is calculated by taking the original FHA base loan amount (the original FHA principal balance excluding financed UFMIP), adding all other financed liens still outstanding, and dividing by the appraised value.

III. Streamline Refinances With an Appraisal (No Credit Qualifying)

a. Maximum Insurable Mortgage Calculation for Streamline Refinances With An Appraisal

The maximum insurable mortgage for streamline refinances with an appraisal is the lesser of:

- the existing principal balance
    - minus the applicable refund of UFMIP
    - plus closing costs, prepaid items to establish the escrow account, and the new UFMIP that will be charged on the refinance transaction, or

- 97.75 percent of the appraised value of the property plus the new UFMIP that will be charged on the refinance.

- The outstanding principal balance
    - may include interest charged by the servicing lender when the payoff is not received on the first day of the month, but
    - may not include delinquent interest, late charges or escrow shortages.

- Prepaid expenses may include:
  - per diem interest to the end of the month on the new loan
  - hazard insurance premium deposits
  - monthly mortgage insurance premiums, and
  - any real estate tax deposits needed to establish the escrow account, regardless of whether the lender refinancing the existing loan is also the servicing lender for that mortgage.

- Discount points may not be included in the new mortgage. If the borrower has agreed to pay discount points, the lender must verify that the borrower has the assets to pay them, along with any other financing costs not included in the new mortgage amount.

b. Policy on Subordinate Financing on Streamline Refinances With An Appraisal

Subordinate liens, including credit lines, regardless of when taken, may remain outstanding, but must be subordinate to the FHA-insured mortgage.

If subordinate financing remains in place, the

- maximum combined loan-to-value (CLTV) is 125 percent, and
- CLTV is based on the new appraised value.

c. Restriction on Borrower Cash Back at Closing on a Streamline Refinance With an Appraisal

A streamline refinance transaction with an appraisal must involve no cash back to the borrower, except for minor adjustments at closing, not to exceed $500.

CHAPTER FIVE

Borrower Eligibility and Credit Analysis

1. Borrower Eligibility Requirements

I. Borrower, Co-borrower and Cosigner Eligibility Requirements

a. Who Is Eligible for FHA Mortgage Insurance

FHA insures mortgages made:

- to individuals with a valid Social Security number (SSN), and
- under the conditions described in this section, to
    - state and local government agencies, and
    - approved nonprofit organizations.

Note: Employees of the World Bank, foreign embassies, etc., may not be required to have an SSN. Conclusive evidence of this exception must be provided.

b. Borrower Age Limits

There is no maximum age limit for a borrower. The minimum age is the age for which a mortgage note can be legally enforced in the state, or other jurisdiction where the property is located.

c. Determination of Credit Worthiness and Minimum Credit Score Requirement

When determining the mortgage creditworthiness of borrowers, co-borrowers, or cosigners, the underwriter takes the following into consideration:
- income
- assets
- liabilities, and
- credit history.

Borrowers with decision credit scores below 500 and with loan-to-value ratios at or above 90 percent are not eligible for FHA-insured mortgage financing.

d. Borrower and Co-borrower Requirements

Both occupying and non-occupying borrowers and co-borrowers:
- take title to the property at settlement
- are obligated on the mortgage note, and
- must sign all security instruments.

e. Cosigner Requirements

Cosigners:
- do not hold ownership interest in a property
- are obligated on the mortgage note and liable for repaying the obligation, and
- must complete and sign all loan documents except the security instruments.

f. Additional Borrower and Co-borrower Eligibility

The table below describes additional requirements and conditions for co-borrowers and cosigners.

Condition/Requirement	Description
Financial Interest Prohibited	A party who has a financial interest in the mortgage loan transaction, such as the seller, builder, or real estate agent, may not be a co-borrower or a cosigner. **Exception:** Exceptions may be granted when the party with the financial interest is related to the borrower by blood, marriage, or law.
Basic Ineligibility for Participation	An individual signing the loan application must not be otherwise ineligible for participation in the mortgage loan transaction. **Note:** This condition applies to all borrowers, regardless of occupancy status.
Principal United States (U.S.) Residence	Non-occupying co-borrowers or cosigners must have a principle residence in the U.S., unless exempted • due to military service with overseas assignments, or • as a U.S. citizen living abroad.

g. Military Personnel Eligibility

Military personnel are considered occupant-owners, and eligible for maximum financing if a member of the immediate family will occupy a property as the principal residence, whether or not the military person is stationed elsewhere.

h. Veteran Eligibility Documentation Requirements

A completed Certificate of Veteran Status (CVS, VA Form 26-8261) issued to a veteran borrower is the only document that may be used for program eligibility. The Department of Veterans Affairs is solely responsible for determining eligibility for a CVS and its subsequent issuance.

Requests for a CVS must be sent on VA Form 26-8261a, along with proof of military service, to the appropriate VA Eligibility Center. This form is available at http://www.va.gov/vaforms/.

i. Title Issues Regarding Non- Borrowing Spouses or Other Parties in Interest

If two or more parties have an ownership interest in the property, but one of the parties is applying for the loan (and credit qualifies for the loan on his/her own), it is not required that the non-applicant individual(s) execute the mortgage note and mortgage, deed of trust, or security deed.

The lender is still required to ensure a valid and enforceable first lien on the property under applicable State law, which may require the execution of the mortgage, deed of trust, or security deed (but typically not the note) by all parties who have an ownership interest in the property.

If the party in question executes the mortgage, deed of trust, or security deed only and not the note, he/she is not considered a borrower for FHA purposes, and therefore need not sign the loan application or be considered in credit underwriting.

II. Ineligible Borrowers

a. Reasons for Mandatory Rejection of a Borrower

A borrower seeking to obtain an FHA-insured mortgage must be rejected if he/she is

- suspended, debarred, or otherwise excluded from participation in HUD's programs and appears on either the
  - HUD Limited Denial of Participation (LDP) list, or
  - General Services Administration's (GSA's) " List of Parties Excluded from Federal Procurement or Non-procurement Programs," or
- presently delinquent on any Federal debt or has a lien placed against his/her property for a debt owed to the United States Government.

Notes:
- A borrower who is delinquent on a Federal debt may become eligible once he/she brings the account current or enters into a satisfactory repayment plan with the Federal agency.

- A mortgage loan is not eligible for insurance if any party involved in the transaction is on either of the above lists. An exception exists for a seller on the list who is selling his/her principal residence.

b. Waiting Period for Borrowers With Past Delinquencies and Defaults

FHA has a three-year waiting period to regain eligibility for another FHA-insured mortgage when the borrower has had past delinquencies or has defaulted on an FHA-insured loan.

The three-year waiting period begins when FHA pays the initial claim to the lender. This includes deed-in-lieu of foreclosure, as well as judicial and other forms of foreclosures.

Lenders should contact the HOC having jurisdiction over the area where the property subject to default is located for information such as the:
• date the claim was paid, and
• date of the initial default.

c. Lender Responsibility for Borrower Screening

Lenders are responsible for screening all borrowers using HUD's Credit Alert Interactive Voice Response System (CAIVRS). A borrower is not eligible for an FHA-insured mortgage if CAIVRS indicates that the borrower:
• is presently delinquent, or
• has had a claim paid within the previous three years on a loan made or insured by FHA.

III. Citizenship and Immigration Status

a. Residency Requirements

U.S. citizenship is not required for mortgage eligibility.

The lender must determine residency status of the borrower, based on:
• information provided on the loan application, and
• other applicable documentation.

b. Lawful Permanent Resident Aliens

FHA insures mortgages for borrowers with lawful permanent resident alien status using the same terms and conditions as those for U.S. citizens.

The mortgage file must:
• include evidence of the permanent residency, and
• indicate that the borrower is a lawful permanent resident alien on the Uniform Residential Loan Application (URLA).

> **Note:** The U.S. Citizenship and Immigration Services (USCIS) within the Department of Homeland Security provides evidence of lawful, permanent residency status.

c. Non- Permanent Resident Aliens

FHA insures mortgages made to non-permanent resident aliens provided that the:
- property will be the borrower's principal residence
- borrower has a valid SSN, and
- borrower is eligible to work in the U.S., as evidenced by an EAD issued by the USCIS.

Note: The Social Security card cannot be used as evidence of work status.

d. EAD Required as Evidence of Work Status

Although Social Security cards may indicate work status, such as "not valid for work purposes," an individual's work status may change without the change being reflected on the actual Social Security card. For this reason, the Social Security card must not be used as evidence of work status, and the EAD must be used instead.

If the EAD will expire within one year and a prior history of residency status renewals exists, the lender may assume that continuation will be granted. If there are not prior renewals, the lender must determine the likelihood of renewal, based on information from the USCIS.

Note: Borrowers residing in the U.S. by virtue of refugee or asylee status granted by the USCIS are automatically eligible to work in this country. An EAD is not required.

e. Non- Lawful Residency

Non-U.S. citizens that do not have lawful residency in the U.S. are not eligible for FHA-insured mortgages.

IV. Living Trusts

a. Property Held in Living Trusts

Property held in a living trust is eligible for FHA mortgage insurance when an individual borrower remains the beneficiary and occupies the property as a principal residence.

The lender must be satisfied that the trust provides reasonable means to assure that the lender will be notified of any changes to the trust regarding occupancy changes, or transfer of beneficial interest.

b. Living Trusts and Security Instruments

The name of the living trust must appear on the security instrument, such as the mortgage, deed of trust, or security deed.

The individual borrower must appear on the security instrument when required to create a valid lien under State law. The owner-occupant, and other borrowers if any, must also appear on the Note with the trust. The individual borrower is not required to appear on the property deed or title.

V. Non-Purchasing Spouses

a. Valid First Liens

If required by State law in order to perfect a valid and enforceable first lien, the non-purchasing spouse may be required to sign either the security instrument or documentation indicating that the individual is relinquishing all rights to the property.

When the security instrument is executed for this reason, the non-purchasing spouse is:
- not considered a borrower, and
- not required to sign the loan application.

Note: Non-applicant individuals can have an ownership interest in the property at the time of settlement without executing the mortgage note and mortgage, deed of trust, or security deed, regardless of whether the transaction is a purchase or a refinance.

b. Non- Purchasing Spouse Debt

Except for obligations specifically excluded by State law, the debts of non-purchasing spouses must be included in the borrower's qualifying ratios, if the:
- borrower resides in a community property state, or
- property being insured is located in a community property state.

c. Non- Purchasing Spouse Credit History

The non-purchasing spouse's credit history is not considered a reason to deny a loan application. However, the non-purchasing spouse's obligations must be considered in the debt-to-income ratio unless excluded by State law. A credit report that complies with the requirements of HUD 4155.1 4.C.2 must be provided for the non-purchasing spouse in order to determine the debts that must be counted in the debt-to-income ratio.

> **Note:** This requirement is applicable if the subject property or the borrower's principal residence is located in a community property state.

VI. Eligibility Requirements for Nonprofit Organizations and State and Local Government Agencies

a. General Policy on the Eligibility of Nonprofit Organizations

Nonprofit organizations are eligible to purchase rental properties with FHA-insured mortgages, provided that they:
- intend to sell or lease the property to low- or moderate-income individuals (generally defined as income not exceeding 115 percent of the applicable median income), and
- meet the requirements for HUD approval

Nonprofit organizations may only obtain FHA-insured fixed rate mortgages. Only an existing FHA-insured mortgage is eligible for refinancing and may never result in equity withdrawal.

b. Percentage of Financing Available

Nonprofit organizations are eligible for the same percentage of financing available on owner-occupied principal residences.

c. HOC and DE Lender Responsibilities for Determining Eligibility and Verifying HUD Approval

The appropriate HOC is responsible for determining a nonprofit organization's eligibility to participate in FHA programs.

The DE lender is responsible for determining:
- the organization's financial capacity for repayment, and
- that the organization, at the time of underwriting, is approved by HUD as a participating nonprofit organization.

Note: Lenders can verify nonprofit approval status by visiting the HUD Web site at hud.gov

d. Requirements for Nonprofit Approval by HUD

HUD must approve the nonprofit organization for it to be eligible to:
- purchase properties with
  - FHA-insured mortgages, and
  - the same percentage of financing available to owner-occupants, and
- provide secondary financing.

In order to receive HUD approval, the nonprofit organization must:
- be of the type described in Section 501(c)(3) as exempt from taxation under Section 501(a) of the Internal Revenue Code of 1986
- have a voluntary board, and no part of the net earnings of the organization or funds from the transaction may benefit any board member, founder, contributor, or individual, and
- have two years' experience as a provider of housing for low and moderate-income persons.

e. Nonprofit Organizations Not Meeting HUD Approval Requirements

A nonprofit organization not meeting any of the requirements, including religious and charitable organizations, may only purchase properties backed by FHA mortgage insurance.

Note: Questions concerning a nonprofit organization's approval should be directed to the appropriate HOC.

f. Eligibility of State and Local Government Agencies

State and local government agencies involved in the provision of housing may obtain FHA-insured

financing provided that the agency provides evidence from its legal counsel that:
- the agency has the legal authority to become the borrower
- the particular state or local government is not in bankruptcy, and
- there is no legal prohibition that would prevent the lender from obtaining a deficiency judgment (if permitted by State law for other types of borrowers) on FHA's behalf in the event of foreclosure or deed-in-lieu of foreclosure.

Loan applications from entities meeting the above requirements may be processed under the DE program without prior approval from the appropriate HOC.

Note: FHA does not require credit reports, financial statements, bank statements, or CAIVRS/LDP/GSA checks.

VII. Eligibility for Federally Related Credit

a. Basis for Rejecting a Borrower for Federally Related Credit

A borrower is not eligible to participate in FHA-insured mortgage transactions if he/she is suspended, debarred, or otherwise excluded from participating in the HUD programs.

A lender must reject a borrower from participation if he/she is on the:
- HUD Limited Denial of Participation (LDP) list
- U.S. General Services Administration (GSA) List of Parties Excluded from Federal Procurement or Non-procurement Programs, and/or
- HUD's Credit Alert Interactive Voice Response System (CAIVRS)

Note: A borrower must also be rejected if he/she is presently delinquent on any Federal debt or has a lien placed against his/her property for a debt owed to the United States Government.

b. Ineligible Mortgage Transactions

A mortgage loan application is not eligible for FHA mortgage insurance if the name of any of the following parties to the mortgage transaction is found on the HUD LDP list or the GSA List of Parties Excluded from Federal Procurement or Non-procurement Programs:
- borrower
- loan officer
- seller
- listing or selling real estate agent

Exception: A seller on the GSA list is exempt if the property being sold is the seller's principal residence.

c. Lender Responsibility for Verifying Borrower Eligibility

To determine whether a borrower is eligible to participate in an FHA mortgage loan transaction or must be rejected, the lender must examine HUD's LDP list and the GSA List of Parties Excluded from Federal Procurement or Non-procurement Programs and document the review on the HUD-92900-LT, FHA Loan Underwriting and Transmittal Summary.

d. Location of the LDP and GSA Lists

The HUD LDP list can be found on the HUD website or on the FHA Connection.

The GSA List of Parties Excluded from Federal Procurement and Non-Procurement Programs can be found at http://epls.arnet.gov or on the FHA Connection.

e. Delinquent Federal Debts

If, after checking public records, credit information, or the Credit Alert Interactive Voice Response System (CAIVRS) a borrower is found to be presently delinquent on any Federal debt or has a lien (including taxes) placed against his/her property for a debt owed to the Federal government, he/she is not eligible for an FHA mortgage until:

- the delinquent account is brought current, paid, or otherwise satisfied, or

- a satisfactory repayment plan is established between the borrower and the Federal agency owed and is verified in writing.

Tax liens may remain unpaid provided the lien holder subordinates the tax lien to the FHA-insured mortgage.

f. Waiting Period for Borrowers With Past Delinquencies and Defaults

FHA has a three-year waiting period to regain eligibility for another FHA-insured mortgage when the borrower has had past delinquencies or has defaulted on an FHA-insured loan.

The three-year waiting period begins when FHA pays the initial claim to the lender. This includes deed-in-lieu of foreclosure, as well as judicial and other forms of foreclosures.

Lenders should contact the HOC having jurisdiction over the area where the property subject to default is located for information such as the:
- date the claim was paid, and
- date of the initial default.

g. Tax Liens Affecting Eligibility for Federally Related Credit

The Internal Revenue Service (IRS) routinely takes a second lien position without the need for independent documentation. For this reason, eligibility for FHA mortgage insurance is not jeopardized by outstanding IRS tax liens remaining on the property, unless the lender has information that the IRS has demanded a first-lien position.

Tax liens may remain unpaid if the lien holder subordinates the tax lien to the FHA-insured mortgage.

Note: If any regular payments are to be made, they must be included in the qualifying ratios.

h. Consideration of a Borrower's Past Payment History on Federally Related Debt

Although a borrower's eligibility for an FHA-insured mortgage may be established by performing the actions described previously in this topic, the overall analysis of the borrower's creditworthiness must:

- consider a borrower's previous failure to make payments to the Federal agency in the agreed-to manner, and

- document the lender's analysis as to how the previous failure does not represent a risk of mortgage default.

VIII. Using Credit Alert Interactive Voice Response System (CAIVRS) to Determine Eligibility for FHA-Insured Mortgage Transactions

a. Description of CAIVRS

The Credit Alert Interactive Voice Response System (CAIVRS) is a Federal government-wide repository of information on:

- those individuals with delinquent or defaulted Federal debt, and
- those for whom a payment of an insurance claim has occurred.

b. Lender Responsibility for Borrower Screening Using CAIVRS

Lenders must use CAIVRS to screen all borrowers (except those involved in a streamline refinance), including nonprofit agencies acting as borrowers. The borrower is not eligible for Federally-related credit, if CAIVRS indicates that he/she:

- is presently delinquent on a Federal debt, or

- has had a claim paid within the previous three years on a loan made and insured on his/her behalf by HUD.

c. Documenting CAIVRS Authorization

Lenders must write the CAIVRS authorization code for each borrower on Form HUD-92900-L, FHA Loan Underwriting and Transmittal Summary.

d. Obtaining Internet Access to CAIVRS

The table below contains guidelines for FHA-approved lenders to use in order to access CAIVRS via the Internet.

Note: As of October 1, 2008, HUD discontinued telephone access to CAIVRS.

If the lender's staff ...	Then ...
currently have FHA Connection User IDs	they should request that their FHA Connection Application Coordinator update their FHA Connection profile to include CAIVRS.
does not have FHA Connection User IDs	they should • access the FHA Connection at https://entp.hud.gov/clas/index.cfm • select Registering to Use the FHA Connection to request a User ID and access to CAIVRS.

Access by Non-FHA Participating Agency Lenders: Non-FHA lender staff should:

• request access from HUD's Internet site at https://entp.hud.gov/caivrs/public/home.html
• select "Registering Lender User ID" from the main menu, and·
• request at least one Application Coordinator User ID, as well as a Standard User ID for each individual user.

e. Exceptions to the Eligibility Rule

The table below describes exceptions to the CAIVRS eligibility rule for an FHA-insured mortgage.

Exception	Description
Legal Assumptions	The borrower is eligible for an FHA-insured mortgage if he/she sold the property, with or without a release of liability, to an individual who subsequently defaulted. The borrower must prove that the loan was current at the time of the assumption.
Divorce	The borrower may be eligible for an FHA-insured mortgage if the divorce decree or legal separation agreement awarded the property and responsibility for payment to the former spouse. The borrower is not eligible if FHA paid a claim on his/her mortgage in default prior to the divorce.

Bankruptcy	The borrower may be eligible for an FHA-insured mortgage if
	
	• the property was included in a bankruptcy caused by circumstances beyond the borrower's control, such as the
	    ■ the death of the principal wage earner, or
	    ■ a serious long-term uninsured illness, and
	
	• the borrower meets the requirements for Chapter 7 bankruptcy, and for Chapter 13 bankruptcy.

Seller Who Is Selling Principal Residence	A mortgage loan is generally not eligible for insurance if any party to the transaction is on either the
	  • (LDP) list, or
	  • General Services Administration's (GSA's) "List of Parties Excluded from Federal Procurement or Non-procurement Programs,"
	
	However, an exception exists for a seller on the GSA list who is selling his/her principal residence.

IMPORTANT: FHA does not require a clear CAIVRS authorization number as a condition for mortgage endorsement. However, the lender must document and justify mortgage approval based on these exceptions.

f. Handling Incorrect CAIVRS Information

FHA may delete erroneous CAIVRS information falsely indicating that a borrower has defaulted on an FHA mortgage, such as incorrect social security number reporting. However, FHA will <u>not</u>

• remove correct CAIVRS information, even if the borrower is judged eligible for Federally-related credit, or

• alter or delete CAIVRS information reported from other Federal agencies, such as the
    ■ Department of Education, or
    ■ Department of Veterans Affairs.

The borrower and/or lender must contact those Federal agencies directly to correct or remove erroneous or outdated information.

g. Lender Responsibility for Resolving Conflicting Information

Lenders may not rely on a clear CAIVRS approval when there is independent evidence of conflicting delinquent Federal obligations. The lenders must:

- document the resolution of any conflicting information, and
- contact the appropriate HOC for instructions or documentation to support the borrower's eligibility if the:
  - CAIVRS message seems erroneous, or
  - date of claim payment needs to be established.

The HOC may provide lenders with:
- information about
  - when the three-year waiting period will elapse
  - erroneous social security numbers, and
- instructions on processing requirements for other-HUD related defaults and claims, such as Title I loans.

2. Property Ownership Requirements and Restrictions

a. What FHA Insures

Except as otherwise stated in this handbook, FHA's single family programs are limited to owner-occupied principal residences only.

b. Description of a Condominium

A condominium is a multi-unit project that:
- has individually-owned units that may be either
  - attached in one or more structures, or
  - detached from each other, and
- is essentially residential in use (for FHA purposes).

A condominium regime is created by state or local law and is characterized by fee simple ownership of a unit which is defined in the condominium documents, together with common areas. The property interest in these areas is both common and undivided on the part of all unit owners, each of whom belong to the Homeowners' Association (HOA) that typically maintains the property and collects assessments or dues from each unit owner.

c. Requirements for Condominium Eligibility

FHA must approve condominium projects before a mortgage on an individual condominium unit can be insured.

> **Exception:** In specific circumstances, a loan on a single unit in an unapproved condominium project, known as a "spot" loan, may qualify for mortgage insurance. The lender must certify that the project satisfies the eligibility criteria for a "spot" loan condominium project that has not been approved by FHA.

d. Seven Unit Limitation for Investors

Entities purchasing investment properties are limited to a financial interest in seven rental dwelling units.

e. Manufactured Housing Condominium Projects (MHCP)

Individual manufactured housing units in condominium projects are eligible for FHA insurance, on both Home Equity Conversion Mortgages (HECM) and forward mortgages. All manufactured housing condominium project (MHCP) approval requests must be processed by the Homeownership Center (HOC) that has authority over the location in which the property is located.

MHCPs may not be processed as site condominiums.

f. Site Condominiums Requirements

Site Condominiums are single family detached dwellings encumbered by a declaration of condominium covenants or condominium form of ownership.

Condominium project approval is not required for Site Condominiums; however, the Condominium Rider must be included in the FHA case binder.

> **Note:** Manufactured housing condominium projects may not be processed as site condominiums.

I. Eligibility Requirements for Principal Residences

a. Definition: Principal Residence

A principal residence is a property that will be occupied by the borrower for the majority of the calendar year.

b. FHA Requirement for Establishing Owner-Occupancy

At least one borrower must occupy the property and sign the security instrument and the mortgage note in order for the property to be considered owner-occupied.

FHA security instruments require a borrower to establish bona fide occupancy in a home as the borrower's principal residence within 60 days of signing the security instrument, with continued occupancy for at least one year.

c. Limitation on Number of FHA- Insured Mortgages Per Borrower

To prevent circumvention of the restrictions on FHA-insured mortgages to investors, FHA generally will not insure more than one principal residence mortgage for any borrower. FHA will not insure a mortgage if it is determined that the transaction was designed to use FHA mortgage insurance as a vehicle for obtaining investment properties, even if the property to be insured will be the only one owned using FHA mortgage insurance.

Any person individually or jointly owning a home covered by an FHA-insured mortgage in which ownership is maintained may not purchase another principal residence with FHA insurance.

Exception: Properties previously acquired as investment properties are not subject to these restrictions.

d. Exceptions to the FHA Policy Limiting the Number of Mortgages Per Borrower

The table below describes the "exception" situations in which FHA does not object to borrowers obtaining multiple FHA-insured mortgages.

Note: Considerations in determining the eligibility of a borrower for one of the exceptions in the table below include the:

> • length of time the previous property was owned by the borrower, and
> • circumstances that compel the borrower to purchase another residence with an FHA-insured mortgage.

d. Exceptions to the FHA Policy Limiting the Number of Mortgages Per Borrower

The table below describes the "exception" situations in which FHA does not object to borrowers obtaining multiple FHA-insured mortgages.

Note: Considerations in determining the eligibility of a borrower for one of the exceptions in the table below include the:

> • length of time the previous property was owned by the borrower, and
> • circumstances that compel the borrower to purchase another residence with an FHA-insured mortgage.

Important: In all cases other than those listed below, the borrower is not eligible to acquire another FHA-insured mortgage until he/she has either:

> • paid off the FHA-insured mortgage on the previous residence, or
> • terminated ownership of that residence.

In all cases other than those listed below, the borrower is not eligible to acquire another FHA-insured mortgage until he/she has either:

> • paid off the FHA-insured mortgage on the previous residence, or
> • terminated ownership of that residence.

Policy Exception	Eligibility Requirements
Relocation	A borrower may be eligible to obtain another mortgage using FHA insurance, without being required to sell an existing property covered by an FHA-insured mortgage, if the borrower is: • relocating, and • establishing residency in an area not with-in reasonable commuting distance from the current principal residence. If the borrower subsequently returns to the area where he/she owns a property with an FHA-insured mortgage, he/she is not required to re-establish primary residency in that property in order to be eligible for another FHA-insured mortgage. *Note:* The relocation need not be employer mandated to qualify for this exception.
Increase in family size	A borrower may be eligible for another home with an FHA-insured mortgage if the number of legal dependents increases to the point that the present house no longer meets the family's needs. The borrower must provide satisfactory evidence: • of the increase in dependents and the property's failure to meet family needs, and • the LTV ratio based on the outstanding mortgage balance and a current appraisal equals 75% or less. If it does not, the borrower must pay the loan down to 75% LTV or less. Note: A current residential appraisal must be used to determine LTV compliance. Tax assessments and market analyses by real estate brokers are not acceptable proof of LTV compliance.
Vacating a jointly owned property	A borrower may be eligible for another FHA-insured mortgage if he/she is vacating a residence that will remain occupied by a co-borrower. Example: An example of an acceptable situation is one in which there is a divorce and the vacating ex-spouse will purchase a new home.
Non-occupying co-borrower	A borrower may be qualified for an FHA-insured mortgage on his/her own principal residence even if he/she is a non-occupying co-borrower with a joint interest in a property being purchased by other family members as a principal residence with an FHA-insured mortgage.

Important: Under no circumstances may investors use the exceptions described in the table above to circumvent FHA's ban on loans to private investors and acquire rental properties through purportedly purchasing "principal residences."

II. Eligibility Requirements for Secondary Residences

a. Definition: Secondary Residence

A secondary residence is a property that a borrower occupies in addition to his/her principal residence.

b. Requirement for HOC Determination of Undue Hardship

Secondary residences are only permitted when:
- the appropriate HOC agrees that an undue hardship exists, meaning that affordable rental housing that meets the needs of the family is not available for lease in the area or within reasonable commuting distance of work, and the maximum loan amount is 85 percent of the lesser of the appraised value or sales price.

Note: DE lenders are not authorized to grant hardship exceptions. Only the HOC may make the determination that an undue hardship exists.

c. Requesting a Hardship Exception

Any request for a hardship exception must be submitted, in writing, by the lender to the appropriate HOC.

d. Limitation on the Number of Secondary Residences

A borrower may have only one secondary residence at any time.

e. Requirements for Secondary Residences

Secondary residences must meet all of the following requirements:

- the secondary residence must not be a vacation home or be otherwise used primarily for recreational purposes

- the borrower must obtain the secondary residence because of seasonal employment, employment relocation, or other circumstances not related to recreational use of the residence, and

- there must be a demonstrated lack of affordable rental housing meeting the needs of the borrower in the area or within a reasonable commuting distance of the borrower's employment, and the borrower must provide supporting documentation of this, including:
  - a satisfactory explanation by the borrower of the need for a secondary residence and the lack of available rental housing, and

- written evidence from local real estate professionals who verify a lack of acceptable housing in the area.

III. Investment Property Eligibility and Underwriting Requirements

a. Definition: Investment Property

An investment property is a property that is not occupied by the borrower as a principal or secondary residence.

b. Loan Transactions in Which a Private Investor May Obtain an FHA- Insured Mortgage

With permission from the appropriate HOC, private investors, may obtain an FHA-insured mortgage when purchasing HUD Real Estate Owned (REO) properties, or obtaining a streamline refinance without an appraisal.

Note: In HUD REO transactions, owner occupancy is not required when the jurisdictional HOC sells the property and permits the purchaser to obtain FHA-insured financing on the investment property.

c. Underwriting Considerations on Investment Properties

Underwriting considerations on investment properties are listed below.

- Individual investors who credit qualify may assume mortgages made on investment properties. This applies also to investment properties purchased before the 1989 ban on investors that have been subsequently streamline refinanced.

- Adjustable rate mortgages (ARMs) and graduated payment mortgages (GPMs) are not permitted on investment properties.

- For investment properties, FHA will not insure loans made solely in the name of a business entity (such as a corporation, partnership, or sole proprietorship), except for streamline refinances in which the mortgage was originally insured in the name of a business. Additionally, FHA requires that:
    - one or more individuals, along with the business entity or trust, must be analyzed for creditworthiness
    - the individual(s) and business entity or trust must appear on the mortgage note, and
    - if all parties appear on the property deed or title, they must also appear on the security instrument (such as the mortgage, deed of trust, or security deed).
- For purchases of HUD REO properties, owner occupancy is not required when the jurisdictional HOC sells the property and permits the purchaser to obtain FHA-insured financing on the investment property.

- Streamline refinancing without an appraisal is permitted on investment properties.

• Base mortgage calculation is 75% LTV applied to the lesser of the appraised value or the sales price.

d. Seven Unit Limitation for Investors

Qualified investor entities are limited to a financial interest (that is, any type of ownership, regardless of the type of financing) in seven rental dwelling units, when the subject property is part of, adjacent to, or contiguous to, a property, subdivision or group of properties owned by the investor.

> The units that count toward this limitation include:
> • each dwelling unit in a two, three, and four family property, and
> • the rental units in an owner-occupied two, three, or four unit property.

Notes: • The lender is responsible for ensuring compliance with this regulation.
• Waivers to the seven unit limitation can only be initiated by the jurisdictional HOC for good cause.

e. Restriction on Investment Properties for Hotel and Transient Use

Investors must assure FHA that investment properties purchased will not be used for hotel or transient purposes, or otherwise rented for periods of less than 30 days.

Completion of Form HUD 92561, Hotel and Transient Use Certification, provides this assurance and is required on every application for:
• two, three, or four family dwellings, and
• single family dwellings that are one of a group of five or more dwellings held by the same borrower.

3. Borrower Credit Analysis

I. General Guidelines for Analyzing Borrower Credit

a. Past Credit Performance

Past credit performance is the most useful guide to use when:
• determining a borrower's attitude toward credit obligations, and
• predicting a borrower's future actions.

Borrowers who have made payments on previous and current obligations in a timely manner represent a reduced risk. Conversely, if a borrower's credit history, despite adequate income to support obligations, reflects continuous slow payments, judgments, and delinquent accounts, significant compensating factors will be necessary to approve the loan.

b. Analyzing Credit History

When analyzing a borrower's credit history, examine the overall pattern of credit behavior, not just isolated occurrences of unsatisfactory or slow payments.

A period of past financial difficulty does not necessarily make the risk unacceptable, if the borrower has maintained a good payment record for a considerable time period since the financial difficulty.

c. Documenting an Analysis of Delinquent Accounts

The lender must document the analysis of delinquent accounts, including whether late payments were based on:
- a disregard for financial obligations
- an inability to manage debt, or
- factors beyond the borrower's control, such as
  - delayed mail delivery, or
  - disputes with creditors.

Minor derogatory information occurring two or more years in the past does not require an explanation. Major indications of derogatory credit, such as judgments, collections, and other recent credit problems, require sufficient written explanation from the borrower. The explanation must make sense, and be consistent with other credit information in the file.

TOTAL Scorecard Accept/Refer Recommendation

The TOTAL Scorecard Accept recommendation does not require an explanation for adverse credit, or other derogatory information; however, there must be evidence of payoff for any outstanding judgments shown on the credit report.

The TOTAL Scorecard Refer recommendation requires an explanation for major indications of derogatory credit, such as:
- judgments and collections, and
- any minor indications within the past two years.

d. Developing a Credit History

The lack of a credit history, or the borrower's decision to not use credit, may not be used as the basis for rejecting the loan application.

Some prospective borrowers may not have an established credit history. For these borrowers, including those who do not use traditional credit, the lender must obtain a non traditional merged credit report (NTMCR) from a credit reporting company or develop a credit history from:
- utility payment records
- rental payments
- automobile insurance payments, and
- other means of direct access from the credit provider.

TOTAL Scorecard Accept Recommendation

If TOTAL Scorecard has issued an Accept recommendation, additional development of credit history is not required.

e. Verifying and Documenting Non Traditional Credit Providers

Only if a NTMCR does not exist or such a service is unavailable may a lender choose to obtain independent verification of credit references. Lenders must document that the providers of non traditional credit do exist, and verify the credit information. Documents confirming the existence of a non traditional credit provider may include:
- public records from the state, county, or city, or
- other documents providing a similar level of objective information.

To verify credit information, lenders must use a published address or telephone number for the credit provider and not rely solely on information provided by the applicant.

Rental references from management companies with payment history for the most recent 12 months may be used in lieu of 12 months cancelled checks. Credit references may also be developed via independent verification directly to the creditor. If a method other than NTMCR is used to verify credit information or rental references, all references obtained from individuals should be backed up with the most recent 12 months cancelled checks

f. Non Traditional Mortgage Credit Report

Lenders may use a non traditional mortgage credit report developed by a credit reporting agency as an alternative method for developing a credit history. Use of this type of report requires that the credit reporting agency has verified:
- the existence of the credit providers
- that the non-traditional credit was actually extended to the borrower, and
- the creditor has a published address or telephone number.

II. Guidelines for Credit Report Review

a. Hierarchy of Credit Review

The basic hierarchy for evaluating credit involves reviewing how payments were made on the following:
- previous housing expenses, including utilities, then
- payment history on installment debts, then
- payment history on revolving accounts.

Generally, a borrower is considered to have an acceptable credit history if he/she does not have late housing or installment debt payments, unless there is major derogatory credit on his/her revolving accounts.

b. Reviewing Previous Rental or Mortgage Payment History

The borrower's housing obligation payment history holds significant importance when evaluating credit. The lender must determine the borrower's housing obligation payment history through the:

- credit report
- verification of rent directly from the landlord (for landlords with no identity-of-interest with the borrower)
- verification of the mortgage directly from the mortgage servicer, or
- the review of canceled checks that cover the most recent 12-month period.

Note: The lender must verify/document the previous 12 months housing history even if the borrower states he/she is living rent free.

TOTAL Scorecard Accept Recommendation - Waive the housing/rental history requirement.

c. Recent and/ or Undisclosed Debts and Inquiries

Lenders must determine the purpose of any recent debts as the indebtedness may have been incurred to obtain the required cash investment.

A borrower must provide a satisfactory explanation for any significant debt that is shown on the credit report, but not listed on the loan application. Written explanation is required for all inquiries shown on the credit report for the last 90 days.

TOTAL Scorecard Accept Recommendation

- Verify the actual monthly payment amount.
- Include the monthly payment amount and resubmit the loan if the liability is greater than $100 per month.
- Determine that any funds borrowed were not/will not be used for the homebuyer's cash investment in the transaction.

Note: Explanation is not required for inquiries.

d. Collections and Judgments

Collections and judgments indicate a borrower's regard for credit obligations, and must be considered in the creditworthiness analysis.

The lender must document reasons for approving a mortgage when the borrower has collection accounts or judgments. The borrower must explain, in writing, all collections and judgments.

TOTAL Scorecard Accept Recommendation

Collection accounts trigger neither an explanation requirement nor a hypothetical monthly payment to be used in qualifying borrowers. The presence of collection accounts in the borrower's credit history already result in lowering the credit bureau scores used in TOTAL and, thus, no further information need be provided by the borrower.

e. Paying off Collections and Judgments

FHA does not require that collection accounts be paid off as a condition of mortgage approval. However, court-ordered judgments must be paid off before the mortgage loan is eligible for FHA insurance endorsement.

Exception: An exception on a court-ordered judgment may be made if the borrower:

- has an agreement with the creditor to make regular and timely payments, and
- has provided documentation indicating that payments have been made according to the agreement.

TOTAL Scorecard Accept/Refer Recommendation

TOTAL Scorecard Accept and Refer recommendations require that the lender obtain evidence of payoff for any outstanding judgments shown on the credit report.

f. Previous Mortgage Foreclosure

A borrower is generally not eligible for a new FHA-insured mortgage when, during the previous three years
- his/her previous principal residence or other real property was foreclosed, or
- he/she has given a deed-in-lieu of foreclosure.

Exception: The lender may grant an exception to the three-year requirement if the foreclosure was the result of documented extenuating circumstances that were beyond the control of the borrower, such as a serious illness or death of a wage earner, and the borrower has re-established good credit since the foreclosure. Divorce is not considered an extenuating circumstance. However, the situation in which a borrower whose loan was current at the time of a divorce in which the ex-spouse received the property and the loan was later foreclosed qualifies as an exception.

Note: The inability to sell the property due to a job transfer or relocation to another area does not qualify as an extenuating circumstance.

g. Chapter 7 Bankruptcy

A Chapter 7 bankruptcy (liquidation) does not disqualify a borrower from obtaining an FHA-insured mortgage, if at least two years have elapsed since the date of the discharge of the bankruptcy. During this time, the borrower must:
- have reestablished good credit, or
- chosen not to incur new credit obligations.

An elapsed period of less than two years, but not less than 12 months may be acceptable for an FHA-insured mortgage, if the borrower:

- can show that the bankruptcy was caused by extenuating circumstances beyond his/her control, and has since exhibited a documented ability to manage his/her financial affairs.

Note: The lender must document that the borrower's current situation indicates that the events that led to the bankruptcy are not likely to recur.

h. Chapter 13 Bankruptcy

A Chapter 13 bankruptcy does not disqualify a borrower from obtaining an FHA-insured mortgage, provided that the lender documents that:

- one year of the payout period under the bankruptcy has elapsed, and
- the borrower's payment performance has been satisfactory and all required payments have been made on time.

The borrower must receive written permission from the court to enter into the mortgage transaction.

TOTAL Scorecard Accept Recommendation

Lender documentation must show two years from the discharge date of a Chapter 13 bankruptcy.

If the Chapter 13 bankruptcy has not been discharged for a minimum period of 2 years, the loan must be downgraded to a Refer and be evaluated by a Direct Endorsement (DE) underwriter.

i. Consumer Credit Counseling Payment Plans

Participating in a consumer credit counseling program does not disqualify a borrower from obtaining an FHA mortgage, provided the lender documents that:

- one year of the pay-out period has elapsed under the plan, and
- the borrower's payment performance has been satisfactory and all required payments have been made on time.

The borrower must receive written permission from the counseling agency to enter into the mortgage transaction.

TOTAL Scorecard Accept Recommendation

The borrower's decision to participate in consumer credit counseling does not trigger a requirement for additional documentation since the credit scores already reflect the degradation in credit history. The borrower's credit history, not voluntary participation in consumer credit counseling, is the important variable in scoring the mortgage and, thus, no explanation or other documentation is needed.

j. Use of Truncated SSNs on Credit Reports

In an effort to reduce the risk of identity theft and other forms of financial fraud, some providers of consumer credit reports have begun using a truncated version of an individual's Social Security Number (SSN) on the credit report product that is offered.

A truncated SSN, that contains as few as the last four digits of a borrower's full number, is acceptable for FHA mortgage insurance purposes provided that:

- the loan application captures the full 9-digit SSN, and
- the borrower's name, SSN and date of birth are validated through the FHA Connection or its functional equivalent.

k. Short Sales

A borrower is not eligible for a new FHA-insured mortgage if s/he pursued a short sale agreement on his or her principal residence simply to:
- take advantage of declining market conditions, and
- purchase at a reduced price a similar or superior property within a reasonable commuting distance.

Borrowers Current at the time of Short Sale

A borrower is considered eligible for a new FHA-insured mortgage if, from the date of loan application for the new mortgage:
- all mortgage payments due on the prior mortgage were made within the month due for the 12 month period preceding the short sale, and
- all installment debt payments for the same time period were also made within the month due.

Borrowers in Default at the time of Short Sale

A borrower in default on his or her mortgage at the time of the short sale (or pre-foreclosure sale) is not eligible for a new FHA-insured mortgage for three years from the date of the pre-foreclosure sale.

Note: A borrower who sold his or her property under FHA's pre-foreclosure sale program is not eligible for a new FHA-insured mortgage from the date that FHA paid the claim associated with the pre-foreclosure sale.

III. Evaluating Non Traditional Credit and Insufficient Credit

a. Evaluating Non Traditional Credit

When evaluating borrowers with non traditional credit histories, a satisfactory credit history, at least 12 months in duration, must include:

- no history of delinquency on rental housing payments
- no more than one 30-day delinquency on payments due to other creditors, and
- no collection accounts/court records reporting (other than medical) filed within the past 12 months.

b. Evaluating Borrowers With Insufficient Credit

When evaluating borrowers with no credit references, or otherwise having only Group II references, a satisfactory credit history, at least 12 months in duration, must include:
- no more than one 30-day delinquency on payments due to any Group II reference, and
- no collection accounts/court records reporting (other than medical) filed within the past 12 months.

c. Underwriting Guidance for Borrowers With Insufficient Credit

In order to enhance the likelihood of homeownership sustainability for borrowers with insufficient credit histories, the underwriting guidance below is provided.

- Qualifying ratios are to be computed only on those occupying the property and obligated on the loan, and may not exceed 31 percent for the payment-to-income ratio and 43 percent for the total debt-to-income ratio. Compensating factors are not applicable for borrowers with insufficient credit references.

- Borrowers should have two months of cash reserves following mortgage loan settlement from their own funds (no cash gifts from any source should be counted in the cash reserves for borrowers in this category).

IV. Borrower Liabilities: Recurring Obligations

a. Types of Recurring Obligations

Recurring obligations include:

- all installment loans
- real estate loans
- child support
- revolving charge accounts
- alimony
- other continuing obligations.

b. Debt to Income Ratio Computation for Recurring Obligations

The lender must include the following when computing the debt to income ratios for recurring obligations:
- monthly housing expense, and
- additional recurring charges extending ten months or more, such as
  - payments on installment accounts
  - child support or separate maintenance payments

- revolving accounts, and
- alimony.

Debts lasting less than ten months must be included if the amount of the debt affects the borrower's ability to pay the mortgage during the months immediately after loan closing, especially if the borrower will have limited or no cash assets after loan closing.

Note: Monthly payments on revolving or open-ended accounts, regardless of the balance, are counted as a liability for qualifying purposes even if the account appears likely to be paid off within 10 months or less.

c. Revolving Account Monthly Payment Calculation

If the credit report shows any revolving accounts with an outstanding balance but no specific minimum monthly payment, the payment must be calculated as the greater of:
- 5 percent of the balance, or
- $10.

Note: If the actual monthly payment is documented from the creditor or the lender obtains a copy of the current statement reflecting the monthly payment, that amount may be used for qualifying purposes.

d. Reduction of Alimony Payment for Qualifying Ratio Calculation

Since there are tax consequences of alimony payments, the lender may choose to treat the monthly alimony obligation as a reduction from the borrower's gross income when calculating qualifying ratios, rather than treating it as a monthly obligation.

V. Borrower Liabilities: Contingent Liability

a. Definition: Contingent Liability

A contingent liability exists when an individual is held responsible for payment of a debt if another party, jointly or severally obligated, defaults on the payment.

b. Application of Contingent Liability Policies

The contingent liability policies described in this topic apply unless the borrower can provide conclusive evidence from the debt holder that there is no possibility that the debt holder will pursue debt collection against him/her should the other party default.

c. Contingent Liability on Mortgage Assumptions

Contingent liability must be considered when the borrower remains obligated on an outstanding FHA-insured, VA-guaranteed, or conventional mortgage secured by property that:
- has been sold or traded within the last 12 months without a release of liability, or
- is to be sold on assumption without a release of liability being obtained.

d. Exemption From Contingent Liability Policy on Mortgage Assumptions

When a mortgage is assumed, contingent liabilities need not be considered if:
- the originating lender of the mortgage being underwritten obtains, from the servicer of the assumed loan, a payment history showing that the mortgage has been current during the previous 12 months, or
- the value of the property, as established by an appraisal or the sales price on the HUD-1 Settlement Statement from the sale of the property, minus the Up-Front Mortgage Insurance Premium (UFMIP) results in an LTV of 75% or less.

e. Contingent Liability on Cosigned Obligations

Contingent liability applies, and the debt must be included in the underwriting analysis, if an individual applying for an FHA-insured mortgage is a cosigner/co-obligor on a:
- car loan
- student loan
- mortgage, or
- any other obligation.

If the lender obtains documented proof that the primary obligor has been making regular payments during the previous 12 months, and does not have a history of delinquent payments on the loan during that time, the payment does not have to be included in the borrower's monthly obligations.

VI. Borrower Liabilities: Projected Obligations and Obligations Not Considered Debt

a. Projected Obligations

Debt payments, such as a student loan or balloon note scheduled to begin or come due within 12 months of the mortgage loan closing, must be included by the lender as anticipated monthly obligations during the underwriting analysis.

Debt payments do not have to be classified as projected obligations if the borrower provides written evidence that the debt will be deferred to a period outside the 12-month timeframe.

Balloon notes that come due within one year of loan closing must be considered in the underwriting analysis.

b. Obligations Not Considered Debt

Obligations not considered debt, and therefore not subtracted from gross income, include
- Federal, state, and local taxes
- Federal Insurance Contributions Act (FICA) or other retirement contributions, such as 401(k) accounts (including repayment of debt secured by these funds)

- commuting costs
- union dues
- child care

- automatic deductions to savings accounts
- open accounts with zero balances
- voluntary deductions.

4. Borrower Employment and Employment Related Income

I. Stability of Income

a. Effective Income

Income may not be used in calculating the borrower's income ratios if it comes from any source that cannot be verified, is not stable, or will not continue.

b. Verifying Employment History

To be eligible for a mortgage, FHA does not require a minimum length of time that a borrower must have held a position of employment. However, the lender must verify the borrower's employment for the most recent two full years, and the borrower must:

- explain any gaps in employment that span one or more months, and

- indicate if he/she was in school or the military for the recent two full years, providing evidence supporting this claim, such as:
  - college transcripts, or
  - discharge papers.

Allowances can be made for seasonal employment, typical for the building trades and agriculture, if documented by the lender.

TOTAL Scorecard Accept Recommendation

The TOTAL Scorecard Accept recommendation does not require an explanation for gaps in employment of six months or less, during the most recent two years.

Note: A borrower with a 25 percent or greater ownership interest in a business is considered self employed and will be evaluated as a self employed borrower for underwriting purposes.

c. Analyzing a Borrower's Employment Record

When analyzing the probability of continued employment, lenders must examine:
- the borrower's past employment record
- qualifications for the position
- previous training and education, and
- the employer's confirmation of continued employment.

Favorably consider a borrower for a mortgage if he/she changes jobs frequently within the same line of work, but continues to advance in income or benefits. In this analysis, income stability takes precedence over job stability.

d. Borrowers Returning to Work After an Extended Absence

A borrower's income may be considered effective and stable when recently returning to work after an extended absence if he/she:

- is employed in the current job for six months or longer, and

- can document a two year work history prior to an absence from employment using
  - traditional employment verifications, and/or
  - copies of W-2 forms or pay stubs.

Note: An acceptable employment situation includes individuals who took several years off from employment to raise children, then returned to the workforce.

Important: Situations not meeting the criteria listed above may only be considered as compensating factors. Extended absence is defined as six months.

II. Salary, Wage and Other Forms of Income

a. General Policy on Borrower Income Analysis

The income of each borrower who will be obligated for the mortgage debt must be analyzed to determine whether his/her income level can be reasonably expected to continue through at least the first three years of the mortgage loan.

In most cases, a borrower's income is limited to salaries or wages. Income from other sources can be considered as effective, when properly verified and documented by the lender.

Notes: Effective income for borrowers planning to retire during the first three-year period must include the amount of:
- documented retirement benefits
- Social Security payments, or
- other payments expected to be received in retirement.

- Lenders must not ask the borrower about possible, future maternity leave.

b. Overtime and Bonus Income

Overtime and bonus income can be used to qualify the borrower if he/she has received this income for the past two years, and it will likely continue. If the employment verification states that the overtime and bonus income is unlikely to continue, it may not be used in qualifying.

The lender must develop an average of bonus or overtime income for the past two years. Periods of overtime and bonus income less than two years may be acceptable, provided the lender can justify and document in writing the reason for using the income for qualifying purposes.

c. Establishing an Overtime and Bonus Income Earning Trend

The lender must establish and document an earnings trend for overtime and bonus income. If either type of income shows a continual decline, the lender must document in writing a sound rationalization for including the income when qualifying the borrower.

A period of more than two years must be used in calculating the average overtime and bonus income if the income varies significantly from year to year.

d. Qualifying Part-Time Income

Part-time and seasonal income can be used to qualify the borrower if the lender documents that the borrower has worked the part-time job uninterrupted for the past two years, and plans to continue. Many low and moderate income families rely on part-time and seasonal income for day to day needs, and lenders should not restrict consideration of such income when qualifying these borrowers.

Part-time income received for less than two years may be included as effective income, provided that the lender justifies and documents that the income is likely to continue.
Part-time income not meeting the qualifying requirements may be considered as a compensating factor only.

Note: For qualifying purposes, "part-time" income refers to employment taken to supplement the borrower's income from regular employment; part-time employment is not a primary job and it is worked less than 40 hours.

e. Income From Seasonal Employment

Seasonal income is considered uninterrupted, and may be used to qualify the borrower, if the lender documents that the borrower:
  • has worked the same job for the past two years, and
  • expects to be rehired the next season.

Seasonal employment includes:
  • umpiring baseball games in the summer, or
  • working at a department store during the holiday shopping season.

f. Primary Employment Less Than 40 Hour Work Week

When a borrower's primary employment is less than a typical 40-hour work week, the lender should evaluate the stability of that income as regular, on-going primary employment.

Example: A registered nurse may have worked 24 hours per week for the last year. Although this job is less than the 40-hour work week, it is the borrower's primary employment, and should be considered effective income.

g. Commission Income

Commission income must be averaged over the previous two years. To qualify commission income, the borrower must provide:
- copies of signed tax returns for the last two years, and
- the most recent pay stub.

Commission income showing a decrease from one year to the next requires significant compensating factors before a borrower can be approved for the loan.

Borrowers whose commission income was received for more than one year, but less than two years may be considered favorably if the underwriter can document the likelihood that the income will continue, and soundly rationalize accepting the commission income.

Notes:
- Unreimbursed business expenses must be subtracted from gross income.
- A commissioned borrower is one who receives more than 25 percent of his/her annual income from commissions.
- A tax transcript obtained directly from the IRS may be used in lieu of signed tax returns, and the cost of the transcript may be charged to the borrower.

h. Qualifying Commission Income Earned for Less Than One Year

Commission income earned for less than one year is not considered effective income. Exceptions may be made for situations in which the borrower's compensation was changed from salary to commission within a similar position with the same employer.

A borrower may also qualify when the portion of earnings not attributed to commissions would be sufficient to qualify the borrower for the mortgage.

i. Employer Differential Payments

If the employer subsidizes a borrower's mortgage payment through direct payments, the amount of the payments is considered gross income, and cannot be used to offset the mortgage payment directly, even if the employer pays the servicing lender directly.

j. Retirement Income

Retirement income must be verified from the former employer, or from Federal tax returns. If any retirement income, such as employer pensions or 401(k)s, will cease within the first full three years of the mortgage loan, the income may only be considered as a compensating factor.

k. Social Security Income

Social Security income must be verified by the Social Security Administration or on Federal tax returns. If any benefits expire within the first full three years of the loan, the income source may be considered only as a compensating factor.

Notes:
• The lender must obtain a complete copy of the current awards letter.
• Not all Social Security income is for retirement-aged recipients; therefore, documented continuation is required.
• Some portion of Social Security income may be "grossed up" if deemed nontaxable by the IRS

l. Automobile Allowances and Expense Account Payments

Only the amount by which the borrower's automobile allowance or expense account payments exceed actual expenditures may be considered income.

To establish the amount to add to gross income, the borrower must provide the following:
• IRS Form 2106, Employee Business Expenses, for the previous two years, and
• employer verification that the payments will continue.

If the borrower uses the standard per-mile rate in calculating automobile expenses, as opposed to the actual cost method, the portion that the IRS considers depreciation may be added back to income.

Expenses that must be treated as recurring debt include:
• the borrower's monthly car payment, and
• any loss resulting from the calculation of the difference between the actual expenditures and the expense account allowance.

III. Borrowers Employed by a Family Owned Business

a. Income Documentation Requirement

In addition to normal employment verification, a borrower employed by a family owned businesses are required to provide evidence that he/she is not an owner of the business, which may include:
• copies of signed personal tax returns, or
• a signed copy of the corporate tax return showing ownership percentage.

Note: A tax transcript obtained directly from the IRS may be used in lieu of signed tax returns, and the cost of the transcript may be charged to the borrower

IV. General Information on Self Employed Borrowers & Income Analysis

a. Definition: Self Employed Borrower

A borrower with a 25 percent or greater ownership interest in a business is considered self employed for FHA loan underwriting purposes.

b. Types of Business Structures

There are four basic types of business structures. They include:

- sole proprietorships
- corporations
- partnerships
- limited liability or "S" corporations

c. Minimum Length of Self Employment

Income from self employment is considered stable, and effective, if the borrower has been self employed for two or more years.

Due to the high probability of failure during the first few years of a business, the requirements described in the table below are necessary for borrowers who have been self employed for less than two years.

If the period of self employment is ...	Then ...
between one and two years	to be eligible for a mortgage loan, the individual must have at least two years of documented previous successful employment in the line of work in which the individual is self employed, or in a related occupation. Note: A combination of one year of employment and formal education or training in the line of work in which the individual is self employed or in a related occupation is also acceptable.
less than one year	the income from the borrower may not be considered effective income.

d. General Documentation Requirements for Self Employed Borrowers

Self employed borrowers must provide the following documentation:
- signed, dated individual tax returns, with all applicable tax schedules for the most recent two years
- for a corporation, "S" corporation, or partnership, signed copies of Federal business income tax returns for the last two years, with all applicable tax schedules
- year to date profit and loss (P&L) statement and balance sheet, and
- business credit report for corporations and "S" corporations.

TOTAL Scorecard Accept Recommendation

No business tax returns are required if all of the following conditions are met:

- individual income tax returns show increasing self employed income over two years
- funds to close are not coming from business accounts, and
- the proposed FHA-insured mortgage is not a cash out refinance.

Note: A business credit report for corporations or "S" corporations is not required for the TOTAL Scorecard Accept recommendation.

e. Establishing a Borrower's Earnings Trend

When qualifying a borrower for a mortgage loan, the lender must establish the borrower's earnings trend from the previous two years using the borrower's tax returns.

If a borrower:
- provides quarterly tax returns, the income analysis may include income through the period covered by the tax filings, or
- is not subject to quarterly tax returns, or does not file them, then the income shown on the P&L statement may be included in the analysis, provided the income stream based on the P&L is consistent with the previous years' earnings.

If the P&L statements submitted for the current year show an income stream considerably greater than what is supported by the previous year's tax returns, the lender must base the income analysis solely on the income verified through the tax returns.

If the borrower's earnings trend for the previous two years is downward and the most recent tax return or P&L is less than the prior year's tax return, the borrower's most recent year's tax return or P&L must be used to calculate his/her income.

f. P&L TOTAL Scorecard Accept/Refer Requirements

The TOTAL Scorecard Accept recommendation does not require a P&L and Balance Sheet, unless the income used to qualify the borrower exceeds that of the two-year average, based on tax returns. In such a case, either an audited P&L statement, or signed quarterly tax return is used to support the greater income stream.

The TOTAL Scorecard Refer recommendation requires a P&L and Balance Sheet, or income information directly from the IRS if both of the following conditions exist:
- more that seven months have elapsed since the business tax year's ending date, and
- income to the self employed borrower from each individual business is greater than 5 percent of his/her stable monthly income.

g. Analyzing the Business's Financial Strength

To determine if the business is expected to generate sufficient income for the borrower's needs, the lender must carefully analyze the business's financial strength, including the source of the business's income and general economic outlook for similar businesses in the area.

Annual earnings that are stable or increasing are acceptable, while businesses that show a significant decline in income over the analysis period are not acceptable, even if the current income and debt ratios meet FHA guidelines.

V. Income Analysis: Individual Tax Returns (IRS Form 1040)

a. General Policy on Adjusting Income Based on a Review of IRS Form 1040

The amount shown on a borrower's IRS Form 1040 as adjusted gross income must either be increased or decreased based on the lender's analysis of the individual tax return and any related tax schedules.

b. Guidelines for Analyzing IRS Form 1040

The table below contains guidelines for analyzing IRS Form 1040

IRS Form 1040 Heading	Description
Wages, Salaries and Tips	An amount shown under this heading may indicate that the individual • is a salaried employee of a corporation, or • has other sources of income. This section may also indicate that the spouse is employed, in which case the spouse's income must be subtracted from the borrower's adjusted gross income.
Business Income and Loss (Schedule C)	Sole proprietorship income calculated on Schedule C is business income. Depreciation or depletion may be added back to the adjusted gross income.
Rents, Royalties, Partnerships (Schedule E)	Any income received from rental properties or royalties may be used as income, after adding back any depreciation shown on Schedule E.
Capital Gain and Losses (Schedule D)	Capital gains or losses generally occur only one time, and should not be considered when determining effective income. However, if the individual has a constant turnover of assets resulting in gains or losses, the capital gain or loss must be considered when determining the income. Three years' tax returns are required to evaluate an earning trend. If the trend: • results in a gain, it may be added as effective income, or • consistently shows a loss, it must be deducted from the total income. • Lender must document anticipated continuation of income through verified assets.

Interest and Dividend Income (Schedule B)	This taxable/tax-exempt income may be added back to the adjusted gross income only if it has been received for the past two years, and is expected to continue.
	If the interest-bearing asset will be liquidated as a source of the cash investment, the lender must appropriately adjust the amount.
Farm Income or Loss (Schedule F)	Any depreciation shown on Schedule F may be added back to the adjusted gross income.
IRA Distributions, Pensions, Annuities, and Social Security Benefits	The non-taxable portion of these items may be added back to the adjusted gross income, if the income is expected to continue for the first three years of the mortgage.
Adjustments to Income	Adjustments to income may be added back to the adjusted gross income if they are • IRA and Keogh retirement deductions • penalties on early withdrawal of savings • health insurance deductions, and • alimony payments.
Employee Business Expenses	Employee business expenses are actual cash expenses that must be deducted from the adjusted gross income.

VI. Income Analysis: Corporate Tax Returns (IRS Form 1120)

a. Description: Corporation

A Corporation is a state-chartered business owned by its stockholders.

b. Need to Obtain Borrower Percentage of Ownership Information

Corporate compensation to the officers, generally in proportion to the percentage of ownership, is shown on the:
   • corporate tax return IRS Form 1120, and
   • individual tax returns.

When a borrower's percentage of ownership does not appear on the tax returns, the lender must obtain the information from the corporation's accountant, along with evidence that the borrower has the right to any compensation.

c. Analyzing Corporate Tax Returns

In order to determine a borrower's self employed income from a corporation the adjusted business income must: be determined and multiplied by the borrower's percentage of ownership in the business.

The table below describes the items found on IRS Form 1120 for which an adjustment must be made in order to determine adjusted business income.

Adjustment Item	Description of Adjustment
Depreciation and Depletion	Add the corporation's depreciation and depletion back to the after-tax income.
Taxable Income	Taxable income is the corporation's net income before Federal taxes. Reduce taxable income by the tax liability.
Fiscal Year vs. Calendar Year	If the corporation operates on a fiscal year that is different from the calendar year, an adjustment must be made to relate corporate income to the individual tax return.
Cash Withdrawals	The borrower's withdrawal of cash from the corporation may have a severe negative impact on the corporation's ability to continue operating.

VII. Income Analysis: "S" Corporation Tax Returns (IRS Form 1120S)

a. Description: "S" Corporation

An "S" Corporation is generally a small, start-up business, with gains and losses passed to stockholders in proportion to each stockholder's percentage of business ownership.

Income for owners of "S" corporations comes from W-2 wages, and is taxed at the individual rate. The IRS Form 1120S, Compensation of Officers line item is transferred to the borrower's individual IRS Form 1040.

b. Analyzing "S" Corporation Tax Returns

"S" corporation depreciation and depletion may be added back to income in proportion to the borrower's share of the corporation's income.

In addition, the income must also be reduced proportionately by the total obligations payable by the corporation in less than one year.

IMPORTANT: The borrower's withdrawal of cash from the corporation may have a severe negative impact on the corporation's ability to continue operating, and must be considered in the income analysis.

VIII. Income Analysis: Partnership Tax Returns (IRS Form 1065)

a. Description: Partnership

A Partnership is formed when two or more individuals form a business, and share in profits, losses, and responsibility for running the company. Each partner pays taxes on his/her proportionate share of the partnership's net income.

b. Analyzing Partnership Tax Returns

Both general and limited partnerships report income on IRS Form 1065, and the partners' share of income is carried over to Schedule E of IRS Form 1040.

The lender must review IRS Form 1065 to assess the viability of the business. Both depreciation and depletion may be added back to the income in proportion to the borrower's share of income. Income must also be reduced proportionately by the total obligations payable by the partnership in less than one year.

IMPORTANT: Cash withdrawals from the partnership may have a severe negative impact on the partnership's ability to continue operating, and must be considered in the income analysis.

5. Non-Employment Related Borrower Income

I. Alimony, Child Support, and Maintenance Income

a. Alimony, Child Support and Maintenance Income Criteria

Alimony, child support, or maintenance income may be considered effective, if:
- payments are likely to be received consistently for the first three years of the mortgage
- the borrower provides the required documentation, which includes a copy of the:
  - final divorce decree
  - court order
  - legal separation agreement,
  - voluntary payment agreement

- the borrower can provide acceptable evidence that payments have been received during the last 12 months, such as:
  - cancelled checks
  - tax returns
  - deposit slips
  - court records

Notes:
- Periods less than 12 months may be acceptable, provided the lender can adequately document the payer's ability and willingness to make timely payments.

- Child support may be "grossed up" under the same provisions as non-taxable income sources.

b. TOTAL Scorecard Accept/Refer Recommendation

The TOTAL Scorecard Accept and Refer recommendation for alimony, child support, and maintenance income requires evidence:
- of receipt, using deposits on bank statements or cancelled checks for the most recent three months that support the amount used when qualifying, and
- that the claimed income will continue for at least three years.

For the financial details, use the front and pertinent pages of the divorce decree, settlement agreement and/or court order.

II. Investment and Trust Income

a. Analyzing Interest and Dividends

Interest and dividend income may be used as long as tax returns or account statements support a two-year receipt history. This income must be averaged over the two years.

Subtract any funds that are derived from these sources, and are required for the cash investment, before calculating the projected interest or dividend income.

b. Trust Income

Income from trusts may be used if guaranteed, constant payments will continue for at least the first three years of the mortgage term.

Required trust income documentation includes a copy of the Trust Agreement or other trustee statement, confirming the amount of the trust, frequency of distribution, and duration of payments.

Trust account funds may be used for the required cash investment if the borrower provides adequate documentation that the withdrawal of funds will not negatively affect income. The borrower may use funds from the trust account for the required cash investment, but the trust income used to determine repayment ability cannot be affected negatively by its use.

c. Notes Receivable Income

In order to include notes receivable income to qualify a borrower, he/she must provide:
- a copy of the note to establish the amount and length of payment, and
- evidence that these payments have been consistently received for the last 12 months through deposit slips, cancelled checks, or tax returns.

If the borrower is not the original payee on the note, the lender must establish that the borrower is now a holder in due course, and able to enforce the note.

d. Calculating Qualifying Ratios for Eligible Investment Properties

Follow the steps in the table below to calculate an investment property's income or loss if the property to be insured is an eligible investment property, or sold through FHA's REO program.

Step	Action
1	Subtract the monthly payment (PITI) from the monthly net rental income of the subject property. **Note:** Calculate the monthly net rental by taking the gross rents, and subtracting the 25 percent reduction or the HOC's percentage reduction for vacancies and repairs.

2	Does the calculation in Step 1 yield a positive number? • If yes, add the number to the borrower's monthly gross income. • If no, and the calculation yields a negative number, consider it a recurring monthly obligation.
3	Calculate the mortgage payment-to-income ratio (top or front-end ratio) by dividing the borrower's current housing expense (principal residence) by the monthly gross income. **Note:** The monthly gross income includes any positive cash flow from the subject investment property.
4	Calculate the total fixed payment-to-income ratio (bottom or back-end ratio) by dividing the borrower's total monthly obligations, including any net loss from the subject investment property, by the borrower's total monthly gross income.

III. Military, Government Agency, and Assistance Program Income

a. Military Income

Military personnel not only receive base pay, but often times are entitled to additional forms of pay, such as:
- income from variable housing allowances
- clothing allowances
- flight or hazard pay
- rations, and
- proficiency pay.

These types of additional pay are acceptable when analyzing a borrower's income as long as the probability of such pay to continue is verified in writing. **Note:** The tax-exempt nature of some of the above payments should also be considered.

b. VA Benefits

Direct compensation for service-related disabilities from the Department of Veterans Affairs (VA) is acceptable, provided the lender receives documentation from the VA.

Education benefits used to offset education expenses are not acceptable.

c. Government Assistance Programs

Income received from government assistance programs is acceptable as long as the paying agency provides documentation indicating that the income is expected to continue for at least three years.

If the income from government assistance programs will not be received for at least three years, it may be considered as a compensating factor.

Unemployment income must be documented for two years, and there must be reasonable assurance that this income will continue. This requirement may apply to seasonal employment.

d. Mortgage Credit Certificates

If a government entity subsidizes the mortgage payments either through direct payments or tax rebates, these payments may be considered as acceptable income.

Either type of subsidy may be added to gross income, or used directly to offset the mortgage payment, before calculating the qualifying ratios.

e. Section 8 Home Ownership Vouchers

A monthly subsidy may be treated as income, if a borrower is receiving subsidies under the housing choice voucher home ownership option from a Public Housing Agency (PHA). Although continuation of the home ownership voucher subsidy beyond the first year is subject to Congressional appropriation, FHA has agreed that it will assume, for the purposes of underwriting, that the subsidy will continue for at least three years.

If the borrower is receiving the subsidy directly, the amount received is treated as income. The amount received may also be treated as non taxable income and be "grossed up" by 25 percent, which means that the amount of the subsidy, plus 25 percent of that subsidy may be added to the borrower's income from employment and/or other sources.

Lenders may treat this subsidy as an "offset" to the monthly mortgage payment (that is, reduce the monthly mortgage payment by the amount of the home ownership assistance payment before dividing by the monthly income to determine the payment-to-income and debt-to-income ratios). The subsidy payment must not pass through the borrower's hands.

The assistance payment must be:
- paid directly to the servicing lender, or
- placed in an account that only the servicing lender may access.

Note: Assistance payments made directly to the borrower must be treated as income.

IV. Rental Income

a. Analyzing the Stability of Rental Income

Rent received for properties owned by the borrower is acceptable as long as the lender can document the stability of the rental income through:
- a current lease
- an agreement to lease, or
- a rental history over the previous 24 months that is free of unexplained gaps greater than three months (such gaps could be explained by student, seasonal, or military renters, or property rehabilitation).

A separate schedule of real estate is not required for rental properties as long as all properties are documented on the URLA.

Note: The underwriting analysis may not consider rental income from any property being vacated by the borrower.

b. Rental Income From Borrower Occupied Property

The rent for multiple unit property where the borrower resides in one or more units and charges rent to tenants of other units may be used for qualifying purposes.

Projected rent for the tenant-occupied units only may:
• be considered gross income, only after deducting the HOC's vacancy and maintenance factor, and not be used as a direct offset to the mortgage payment.

c. Income from Roommates in a Single Family Property

Income from roommates in a single family property occupied as the borrower's primary residence is not acceptable. Rental income from boarders however, is acceptable, if the boarders are related by blood, marriage, or law.

The rental income may be considered effective, if shown on the borrower's tax return. If not on the tax return, rental income paid by the boarder:
• may be considered a compensating factor, and
• must be adequately documented by the lender.

d. Documentation Required to Verify Rental Income

Analysis of the following required documentation is necessary to verify all borrower rental income:
• IRS Form 1040 Schedule E, and
• current leases/rental agreements

e. Analyzing IRS Form 1040 Schedule E

The IRS Form 1040 Schedule E is required to verify all rental income. Depreciation shown on Schedule E may be added back to the net income or loss.

Positive rental income is considered gross income for qualifying purposes, while negative income must be treated as a recurring liability.

The lender must confirm that the borrower still owns each property listed, by comparing Schedule E with the real estate owned section of the URLA. If the borrower owns six or more units in the same general area, a map must be provided disclosing the locations of the units as evidence of compliance with FHA's seven-unit limitation.

f. Using Current Leases to Analyze Rental Income

The borrower can provide a current signed lease or other rental agreement for a property that was acquired since the last income tax filing, and is not shown on Schedule E.

In order to calculate the rental income:
- reduce the gross rental amount by 25 percent (or the percentage developed by the jurisdictional HOC) for vacancies and maintenance
- subtract PITI and any homeowners' association dues, and
- apply the resulting amount to
  - income, if positive, or
  - recurring debts, if negative.

g. Exclusion of Rental Income From Property Being Vacated by the Borrower

Underwriters may not consider any rental income from a borrower's principal residence that is being vacated in favor of another principal residence.

Notes:
- This policy assures that a borrower either has sufficient income to make both mortgage payments without any rental income, or has an equity position not likely to result in defaulting on the mortgage on the property being vacated.

- This applies solely to a principal residence being vacated in favor of another principal residence. It does not apply to existing rental properties disclosed on the loan application and confirmed by tax returns (Schedule E of form IRS 1040).

h. Policy Exceptions Regarding the Exclusion of Rental Income From a Principal Residence Being Vacated by a Borrower

When a borrower vacates a principal residence in favor of another principal residence, the rental income, reduced by the appropriate vacancy factor as determined by the jurisdictional FHA HOC, may be considered in the underwriting analysis under the circumstances listed in the table below.

Exception	Description
Relocations	The borrower is relocating with a new employer, or being transferred by the current employer to an area not within reasonable and locally-recognized commuting distance. A properly executed lease agreement (that is, a lease signed by the borrower and the lessee) of at least one year's duration after the loan is closed is required. Note: FHA recommends that underwriters also obtain evidence of the security deposit and/or evidence the first month's rent was paid to the homeowner.

Sufficient Equity in Vacated Property	The borrower has a loan-to-value ratio of 75% percent or less, as determined either by
	• a current (no more than six months old) residential appraisal, or • comparing the unpaid principal balance to the original sales price of the property. Note: The appraisal, in addition to using forms Fannie Mae1004/Freddie Mac 70, may be an exterior-only appraisal using form Fannie Mae/Freddie Mac 2055, and for condominium units, form Fannie Mae1075/Freddie Mac 466.

V. Non Taxable and Projected Income

a. Types of Non Taxable Income

Certain types of regular income may not be subject to Federal tax. Such types of non taxable income include:
- some portion of Social Security, some Federal government employee retirement income, Railroad Retirement Benefits, and some state government retirement income
- certain types of disability and public assistance payments
- child support
- military allowances, and
- other income that is documented as being exempt from Federal income taxes.

b. Adding Non Taxable Income to a Borrower's Gross Income

The amount of continuing tax savings attributed to regular income not subject to Federal taxes may be added to the borrower's gross income.

The percentage of non-taxable income that may be added cannot exceed the appropriate tax rate for the income amount. Additional allowances for dependents are not acceptable.

The lender
- must document and support the amount of income grossed up for any non-taxable income source, and
- should use the tax rate used to calculate the borrower's last year's income tax.

Note: If the borrower is not required to file a Federal tax return, the tax rate to use is 25 percent.

c. Analyzing Projected Income

Projected or hypothetical income is not acceptable for qualifying purposes. However, exceptions are permitted for income from the following sources:

- cost-of-living adjustments
- performance raises
- bonuses

For the above exceptions to apply, the income must be verified in writing by the employer and scheduled to begin within 60 days of loan closing.

d. Projected Income for a New Job

Projected income is acceptable for qualifying purposes for a borrower scheduled to start a new job within 60 days of loan closing if there is a guaranteed, non-revocable contract for employment.

The lender must verify that the borrower will have sufficient income or cash reserves to support the mortgage payment and any other obligations between loan closing and the start of employment. Examples of this type of scenario are teachers whose contracts begin with the new school year, or physicians beginning a residency after the loan closes fall under this category.

The loan is not eligible for endorsement if the loan closes more than 60 days before the borrower starts the new job. To be eligible for endorsement, the lender must obtain from the borrower a pay stub or other acceptable evidence indicating that he/she has started the new job.

6. Borrower Qualifying Ratios

I. General Information on Borrower Qualifying

a. Lender Responsibility When Qualifying a Borrower

The lender is responsible for adequately analyzing the probability that a borrower will be able to repay the mortgage obligation according to the terms of the loan.

This responsibility includes using debt-to-income ratios and compensating factors when qualifying a borrower. Qualifying ratios can be exceeded when significant compensating factors exist.

b. Importance of Careful Underwriting Analysis

Underwriting requires a careful analysis of many aspects of the mortgage. Each loan is a separate and unique transaction, and there may be multiple factors that demonstrate a borrower's ability and willingness to make timely mortgage payments.

Simply establishing that a loan transaction meets minimal standards does not necessarily constitute prudent underwriting. When qualifying a borrower, it is important to avoid the danger of "layering flexibilities" when assessing the mortgage insurance risk.

II. Debt to Income Ratios

a. General Information About Debt to Income Ratios

Debt to income ratios are used to determine whether the borrower can reasonably be expected to

meet the expenses involved in home ownership, and provide for his/her family. In order to make this determination, the lender must complete the following two ratios:
- the Mortgage Payment Expense to Effective Income ratio, and
- the Total Fixed Payment to Effective Income ratio

Note: For loans to be scored through the TOTAL Scorecard, the debt-to-income ratios must be calculated for entry into the Automated Underwriting System (AUS) to be evaluated by TOTAL.

b. Mortgage Payment Expense to Effective Income Ratio

The relationship of the mortgage payment to income is considered acceptable if the total mortgage payment does not exceed 31 percent of the gross effective income.

A ratio exceeding 31 percent may be acceptable only if significant compensating factors are documented and recorded on Form HUD-92900-LT, FHA Loan Underwriting and Transmittal Summary.

For those borrowers who qualify under FHA's Energy Efficient Homes (EEH), the ratio is set at 33 percent. **Note:** The total mortgage payment includes:
- principal and interest
- hazard insurance
- ground rent
- special assessments
- escrow deposits for real estate taxes
- the mortgage insurance premium
- homeowners' association dues
- payments for acceptable secondary financing

c. Total Fixed Payment to Effective Income Ratio

The relationship of total obligations to income is considered acceptable if the total mortgage payment and all recurring charges do not exceed 43 percent of the gross effective income.

A ratio exceeding 43 percent may be acceptable only if significant compensating factors are documented and recorded on Form HUD-92900-LT, FHA Loan Underwriting and Transmittal Summary. For those borrowers who qualify under FHA's EEH, the ratio is set at 45 percent.

d. Estimating Real Estate Taxes When Determining Debt to Income Ratios

For real estate taxes, lenders must use accurate estimates of monthly property tax escrows when qualifying borrowers. In new construction cases, property tax estimates must be based on the land and completed improvements, not just on the land value.

III. Compensating Factors

a. Documentation of the Use of Compensating Factors

Compensating factors that are used to justify approval of mortgage loans with ratios that exceed benchmark guidelines must be recorded on the Underwriter Comments section of Form HUD-92900-LT, FHA Loan Underwriting and Transmittal Summary. Any compensating factor used to justify mortgage approval must also be supported by documentation.

TOTAL Scorecard Accept Recommendation

The TOTAL Scorecard Accept recommendation does not require documented compensating factors, even if qualifying ratios have exceeded FHA benchmark guidelines.

b. Compensating Factors Benchmark Guidelines

The table below describes the compensating factors that may be used to justify approval of mortgage loans with ratios that exceed FHA benchmark guidelines.

Compensating Factor	Guideline Description
Housing Expense Payments	The borrower has successfully demonstrated the ability to pay housing expenses greater than or equal to the proposed monthly housing expenses for the new mortgage over the past 12-24 months.
Down Payment	The borrower makes a large down payment of 10 percent or higher toward the purchase of the property.
Accumulated Savings	The borrower has demonstrated an ability to accumulate savings, and a conservative attitude toward using credit.
Previous Credit History	A borrower's previous credit history shows that he/she has the ability to devote a greater portion of income to housing expenses.
Compensation or Income Not Reflected in Effective Income	The borrower receives documented compensation or income that is not reflected in effective income, but directly affects his/her ability to pay the mortgage. This type of income includes food stamps, and similar public benefits.
Minimal Housing Expense Increase	There is only a minimal increase in the borrower's housing expense.
Substantial Cash Reserves	The borrower has substantial documented cash reserves (at least three months worth) after closing. The lender must judge if the substantial cash reserve asset is liquid or readily convertible to cash, and can be done so absent retirement or job termination, when determining if the asset can be included as cash reserves, or cash to close. Funds and/or "assets" that are not to be considered as cash reserves include equity in other properties and proceeds from a cash-out refinance. Lenders may use a portion of a borrower's retirement account, subject to the conditions stated below. To account for withdrawal penalties and taxes, only 60% of the vested amount of the account may be used. The lender must document the existence of the account with the most recent depository or brokerage account statement. In addition, evidence must be provided that the retirement account allows for withdrawals for conditions other than in connection with the borrower's employment termination, retirement, or death. If withdrawals can only be made under these circumstances, the retirement account may not be included as cash reserves. If any of these funds are also to be used for loan settlement, that amount must be subtracted from the amount included as cash reserves. Similarly, any gift funds that remain in the borrower's account following loan closing, subject to proper documentation, may be considered as cash.

Substantial Non-Taxable Income	The borrower has substantial non-taxable income.
Potential for Increased Earnings	The borrower has a potential for increased earnings, as indicated by job training or education in his/her profession.
Primary Wage-Earner Relocation	The home is being purchased because the primary wage-earner is relocating, and the secondary wage-earner: has an established employment history, is expected to return to work, and has reasonable prospects for securing employment in a similar occupation in the new area. **Note:** The underwriter must document the availability of the potential employment.

CHAPTER SIX

Borrower Funds To Close

1. Settlement Requirements

I. General Information on Settlement Requirements

a. Lender Responsibility for Estimating Settlement Requirements

For each transaction, the lender must provide a Good Faith Estimate (GFE) and HUD-1 Settlement Statement, consistent with the Real Estate Settlement Procedures Act (RESPA) to determine the cash requirements to close the mortgage transaction.

In addition to the minimum down payment, additional borrower expenses must be included in the total amount of cash that the borrower must provide at mortgage settlement. Such additional expenses include, but are not limited to:
- closing costs, such as those customary and reasonable costs necessary to close the mortgage loan
- prepaid items
- discount points
- non-realty or personal property
- up-front mortgage insurance premium (UFMIP) amounts
- repairs and improvements
- real estate broker fees
- mortgage broker fees
- premium pricing on the Federal Housing Administration (FHA) insured mortgages, and
- yield spread premiums.

b. Disclosure Of Origination Charges on the Good Faith Estimate

Lenders must include the sum of all fees and charges from origination-related charges in Box 1 on page 2 of the Good Faith Estimate (GFE).

The figure in Box 1
- represents all compensation to the lender and/or broker for originating the loan
- will most often exceed the specific origination fee caps set for government programs.

Although the GFE requires that lenders provide an aggregated cost for origination services, if a government program or state law requires that lenders provide more detailed information to specific distinct origination fees and charges, lenders may itemize these charges in the empty 800 lines of the HUD-1 Settlement Statement, to the left of the column.

c. Determining the Amount Needed for Closing

The amount of cash needed by the borrower for closing a loan eligible for FHA mortgage insurance is the difference between the total cost to acquire the property and the amount of the FHA-insured mortgage, excluding any UFMIP.

II. Settlement Requirements Needed to Close

a. Origination Fee, Unallowable, and Other Closing Costs

Lenders may charge and collect from borrowers those customary and reasonable costs necessary to close the mortgage loan. Borrowers may not pay a tax service fee.

FHA no longer limits the origination fee to one percent of the mortgage amount for its standard mortgage insurance programs. However, both Home Equity Conversion Mortgage (HECM) and Section 203(k) Rehabilitation Mortgage Insurance programs retain their statutory origination fee caps.

Lenders may charge and collect:
- a supplemental origination fee on Section 203(k) rehabilitation mortgages, or
- two percent on FHA's Home Equity Conversion Mortgages (HECMs).

b. Types of Prepaid Items (Including Per Diem Interest)

Prepaid items are collected at closing to cover
- taxes
- mortgage insurance premiums
- other similar fees and charges
- accrued and unaccrued hazard insurance
- per diem interest

Per Diem Interest

The lender must use a minimum of 15 days of per diem interest when estimating prepaid items. To reduce the burden on borrowers whose loans were scheduled to close at the end of the month, but did not due to unforeseen circumstances, lenders and borrowers may agree to credit the per diem interest to the borrower and have the mortgage payments begin the first of the succeeding month.

c. Discount Points

Discount points that are being paid by the borrower:
- become part of the total cash required to close, and
- are not eligible for meeting the minimum down payment requirement.

d. Non Realty or Personal Property

Non realty (chattel) or personal property items that the borrower agrees to pay for separately, including the amount subtracted from the sales price when determining the maximum mortgage, are included in the total cash requirements for the loan.

e. UFMIP Amounts

Any UFMIP amounts paid in cash are added to the total cash settlement requirements. The UFMIP must be:
- entirely financed into the mortgage, except any amount less than $1.00, or

- paid entirely in cash and all mortgage amounts rounded down to a multiple of $1.00.

f. Repairs and Improvements

Repairs and improvements, or any portion, paid by the borrower that cannot be financed into the mortgage are part of the borrower's total cash requirements.

g. Real Estate Broker Fees

If a borrower is represented by a real estate buyer-broker and must pay any fee directly to the broker, that expense must:

- be included in the total of the borrower's settlement requirements, and

- appear on the HUD-1 Settlement Statement.

If the seller pays the buyer-broker fee as part of the sales commission, it is not considered an inducement to purchase, or part of the 6 percent seller contributions limitation, as long as the seller is paying only the normal sales commission for that market. Any additional seller-paid commission to the buyer-broker is considered an inducement to purchase.

To determine if the seller paid a buyer-broker fee in addition to the normal sales commission for the market, the lender must obtain a copy of the original listing agreement, and compare it with the HUD-1 Settlement Statement.

h. Mortgage Broker Fees

Include mortgage broker fees in the total of the borrower's cash settlement requirements and on the HUD-1 Settlement Statement, if he/she pays a fee directly to a mortgage broker.

This requirement applies only in instances in which the borrower independently engages a mortgage broker exclusively to seek financing, and pays the broker directly. The mortgage broker cannot be the same as the originating lender.

Note: The payment may not come from the lending institution.

i. Premium Pricing on FHA- Insured Mortgages

Lenders may pay the borrower's closing costs, and/or prepaid items by "premium pricing." Closing costs paid in this manner do not need to be included as part of the 6 percent seller contribution limit. The funds derived from a premium priced mortgage:
- may never be used to pay any portion of the borrower's down payment
- must be disclosed on the Good Faith Estimate (GFE) and the HUD-1 Settlement Statement
- must be used to reduce the principal balance if the premium pricing agreement establishes a specific dollar amount for closing cost and prepaid expenses, with any remaining funds in excess of actual costs reverting to the borrower, and
- may not be used for payment of debts, collection accounts, escrow shortages or missed mortgage payments, or judgments.

Note: The GFE and HUD-1 Settlement Statement must contain an itemized statement indicating which items are being paid on the borrower's behalf. It is unacceptable to disclose only a lump sum.

j. Yield Spread Premium

Yield spread premiums (YSP) are not part of the cash required to close, but must be disclosed to borrowers on the GFE and HUD-1 Settlement Statement, in accordance with the Real Estate Settlement Procedures Act (RESPA).

k. Seller Credits on the HUD-1 Settlement Statement

The regulations do not require or permit the presentation or disclosure of seller-paid credits on the Good Faith Estimate (GFE). On the HUD-1 Settlement Statement, the charge will be displayed in the borrower's column on the HUD-1 and a credit to offset charges will be listed in Section J, Summary of Borrower's Transaction on lines 204-209 with a reduction to the seller's proceeds in Section K, Summary of Seller's Transaction on lines 506-509. When the seller contributes to more than one expense, the seller credit shown on the HUD-1 must reflect the lump sum payment.

2. Acceptable Sources of Borrower Funds

I. General Information on Acceptable Sources of Borrower Funds

a. Closing Cost and Minimum Cash Investment Requirements

Under most FHA programs, the borrower is required to make a minimum down payment into the transaction of at least 3.5 percent of the lesser of the appraised value of the property or the sales price.

Additionally, the borrower must have sufficient funds to cover borrower-paid closing costs and fee at the time of settlement. Such funds used to cover the required minimum down payment, as well as closing costs and fees, must come from acceptable sources and must be verified and properly documented.

II. Cash and Savings/Checking Accounts as Acceptable Sources of Funds

a. Earnest Money Deposit

The lender must verify with documentation, the deposit amount and source of funds, if the amount of the earnest money deposit exceeds 2 percent of the sales price, or appears excessive based on the borrower's history of accumulating savings.

> Satisfactory documentation includes:
> - a copy of the borrower's cancelled check
> - certification from the deposit-holder acknowledging receipt of funds, or
> - separate evidence of the source of funds.

Separate evidence includes a verification of deposit (VOD) or bank statement showing that the average balance was sufficient to cover the amount of the earnest money deposit, at the time of the deposit.

b. Savings and Checking Accounts

A VOD, along with the most recent bank statement, may be used to verify savings and checking accounts.

If there is a large increase in an account, or the account was recently opened, the lender must obtain from the borrower a credible explanation of the source of the funds.

TOTAL Scorecard Accept and Refer recommendations require that the lender:
- obtain an explanation and documentation for recent large deposits in excess of 2 percent of the property sales price, and
- verify that any recent debts were not incurred to obtain part, or all, of the required cash investment on the property being purchased.

c. Cash Saved at Home

Borrowers who have saved cash at home, and are able to adequately demonstrate the ability to do so, are permitted to have this money included as an acceptable source of funds to close the mortgage.

To include cash saved at home when assessing the borrower's cash assets, the:
- money must be verified, whether deposited in a financial institution, or held by the escrow/title company and borrower must provide satisfactory evidence of the ability to accumulate such savings.

d. Verifying Cash Saved at Home

Verifying the cash saved at home assets requires the borrower to explain in writing:
- how the funds were accumulated, and
- the amount of time it took to accumulate the funds.

The lender must determine the reasonableness of the accumulation, based on the:
- borrower's income stream
- time period during which the funds were saved
- borrower's spending habits, and
- documented expenses and the borrower's history of using financial institutions.

Note: Borrowers with checking and/or savings accounts are less likely to save money at home, than individuals with no history of such accounts.

e. Cash Accumulated With Private Savings Clubs

Some borrowers may choose to use non-traditional methods to save money by making deposits into private savings clubs. Often, these private savings clubs pool resources for use among the membership.

If a borrower claims that the cash to close an FHA-insured mortgage is from savings held with a private savings club, he/she must be able to adequately document the accumulation of the funds with the club.

f. Requirements for Private Savings Clubs

While private savings clubs are not supervised banking institutions, the clubs must, at a minimum, have: account ledgers, receipts from the club, verification from the club treasurer, and identification of the club.

The lender must reverify the information, and the underwriter must be able to determine that:
- it was reasonable for the borrower to have saved the money claimed, and
- there is no evidence that the funds were borrowed with an expectation of repayment.

III. Investments as an Acceptable Source of Funds

a. IRAs, Thrift Savings Plans, and 401(k)s and Keogh Accounts

Up to 60 percent of the value of assets such as IRAs, thrift savings plans, 401(k) and Keogh accounts may be included in the underwriting analysis, unless the borrower provides conclusive evidence that a higher percentage may be withdrawn, after subtracting any:

- Federal income tax
- withdrawal penalties.

Notes: Redemption evidence is required. The portion of the assets not used to meet closing requirements, after adjusting for taxes and penalties, may be counted as reserves.

TOTAL Scorecard Accept/Reject Recommendation

TOTAL Scorecard Accept or Reject recommendations require the lender to document the terms and conditions for withdrawal and/or borrowing, and that the borrower is eligible for these withdrawals.

Use only 60 percent of the amount in the account, unless the borrower presents documentation supporting a greater amount, after subtracting any taxes or penalties for early withdrawal.

Note: Liquidation evidence is not required.

b. Stocks and Bonds

The monthly or quarterly statement provided by the stockbroker or financial institution managing the portfolio may be used to verify the value of stocks and bonds.

Total Scorecard Accept Recommendation

Evidence of liquidation is not required for the TOTAL Scorecard Accept recommendation.

Note: The actual receipt of funds must be verified and documented.

c. Savings Bonds

Government issued bonds are counted at the original purchase price, unless eligibility for redemption and the redemption value are confirmed.

Note: The actual receipt of funds at redemption must be verified.

IV. Gifts as an Acceptable Source of Funds

a. Description of Gift Funds

In order for funds to be considered a gift there must be no expected or implied repayment of the funds to the donor by the borrower.

Note: The portion of the gift not used to meet closing requirements may be counted as reserves.

b. Who Can Provide a Gift

An outright gift of the cash investment is acceptable if the donor is:

- the borrower's relative
- the borrower's employer or labor union
- a charitable organization
- a governmental agency or public entity that has a program providing home ownership assistance to

- low- and moderate-income families
- first-time homebuyers, or
- a close friend with a clearly defined and documented interest in the borrower.

c. Who Cannot Provide a Gift

The gift donor may not be a person or entity with an interest in the sale of the property, such as

• the seller	• the real estate agent or broker
• the builder	• an associated entity

Gifts from these sources are considered inducements to purchase, and must be subtracted from the sales price.

Note: This applies to properties where the seller is a government agency selling foreclosed properties, such as the US Department of Veterans Affairs (VA) or Rural Housing Services.

d. Lender Responsibility for Verifying the Acceptability of Gift Fund Sources

Regardless of when gift funds are made available to a borrower, the lender must be able to determine that the gift funds were not provided by an unacceptable source, and were the donor's own funds.

When the transfer occurs at closing, the lender is responsible for verifying that the closing agent received the funds from the donor for the amount of the gift, and that the funds were from an acceptable source.

e. Requirements Regarding Donor Source of Funds

As a general rule, FHA is not concerned with how a donor obtains gift funds, provided that the funds are not derived in any manner from a party to the sales transaction.

Donors may borrow gift funds from any other acceptable source, provided the mortgage borrowers are not obligors to any note to secure money borrowed to give the gift.

f. Equity Credit

Only family members may provide equity credit as a gift on property being sold to other family members. The restrictions on gifts previously discussed in this topic and the restriction on equity credit may be waived by the jurisdictional Homeownership Center (HOC), provided that the seller is contributing to or operating an acceptable affordable housing program.

g. Payment of Consumer Debt Must Result in Sales Price Reduction

FHA regards the payment of consumer debt by third parties to be an inducement to purchase.

While FHA permits sellers and other parties to make contributions of up to 6 percent of the sales price of a property toward a buyer's actual closing costs and financing concessions, this requirement applies exclusively to the mortgage financing provision.

When someone other than a family member has paid off debts or other expenses on behalf of the borrower:
- the funds must be treated as an inducement to purchase, and
- there must be a dollar for dollar reduction to the sales price when calculating the maximum insurable mortgage.

Note: The dollar for dollar reduction to the sales price also applies to gift funds not meeting the requirement:
- that the gift be for down payment assistance, and
- that it be provided by an acceptable source.

h. Using Down Payment Assistance Programs

FHA does not "approve" down payment assistance programs providing gifts administered by charitable organizations, such as nonprofits. FHA also does not allow nonprofit entities to provide gifts to pay off:

- installment loans
- collections
- similar debts
- credit cards
- judgments

Lenders must ensure that a gift provided by a charitable organization meets the appropriate FHA requirements, and that the transfer of funds is properly documented.

i. Gifts from Charitable Organizations That Lose or Give Up Their Federal Tax- Exempt Status

If a charitable organization makes a gift that is to be used for all, or part, of a borrower's down payment, and the organization providing the gift loses or gives up its Federal tax exempt status, FHA will recognize the gift as an acceptable source of the down payment provided that:
- the gift is made to the borrower
- the gift is properly documented, and
- the borrower has entered into a contract of sale (including any amendments to purchase price) on, or before, the date the IRS officially announces that the charitable organization's tax exempt status is terminated.

j. Lender Responsibility for Ensuring That an Entity Is a Charitable Organization

The lender is responsible for ensuring that an entity is a charitable organization as defined by Section 501(a) of the Internal Revenue Code (IRC) of 1986 pursuant to Section 501(c) (3) of the IRC.

One resource available to lenders for obtaining this information is the Internal Revenue Service (IRS) Publication 78, Cumulative List of Organizations described in Section 170(c) of the Internal Revenue Code of 1986, which contains a list of organizations eligible to receive tax-deductible charitable contributions.

The IRS has an online version of this list that can help lenders and others conduct a search of these organizations. The online version can be found at http://apps.irs.gov/app/pub78 using the following instructions to obtain the latest update:

- enter search data and click "Search"

- click "Search for Charities" under the "Charities & Non-Profits Topics" heading on the left-hand side of the page

- click "Recent Revocations and Deletions from Cumulative List" under the "Additional Information" heading in the middle of the page, and

- click the name of the organization if the name appears on the list displayed.

In addition, FHA has developed a web page that provides a listing of down payment assistance providers whose nonprofit status has been revoked.

V. Gift Fund Required Documentation

a. Gift Letter Requirement

A lender must document any borrower gift funds through a gift letter, signed by the donor and borrower. The gift letter must:
- show the donor's name, address, telephone number
- specify the dollar amount of the gift, and
- state
  - the nature of the donor's relationship to the borrower, and
  - that no repayment is required.

TOTAL Scorecard Accept/Refer Recommendation

For the TOTAL Scorecard Accept and Refer recommendation, the borrower must list the following:
- name, address, telephone number
- relationship to the home buyer, and
- the dollar amount of the gift on the loan application or in a gift letter for each cash gift received.

If sufficient funds required for closing are not already verified in the borrower's accounts, document the transfer of the gift funds to the borrower's accounts.

b. Documenting the Transfer of Gift Funds

The lender must document the transfer of the gift funds from the donor to the borrower.

The table below describes the requirements for the transfer of gift funds.

If the gift funds ...	Then ...
are in the borrower's account	obtain • a copy of the withdrawal document showing that the withdrawal is from the donor's account, and • the borrower's deposit slip and bank statement showing the deposit.
• are to be provided at closing, and • are in the form of a certified check from the donor's account	obtain a • bank statement showing the withdrawal from the donor's account, and • copy of the certified check.
• are to be provided at closing, and • are in the form of a cashier's check, money order, official check, or other type of bank check	have the donor provide a withdrawal document or cancelled check for the amount of the gift, showing that the funds came from the donor's personal account.
• are to be provided at closing, and • are in the form of an electronic wire transfer to the closing agent	have the donor provide documentation of the wire transfer. **Note:** The lender must obtain and keep the documentation of the wire transfer in its mortgage loan application binder. While the document does not need to be provided in the insurance binder, it must be available for inspection by FHA's Quality Assurance Division (QAD) when that office conducts its onsite review of lenders.
• are being borrowed by the donor, and • documentation from the bank or other savings account is not available	have the donor provide written evidence that the funds were borrowed from an acceptable source, not from a party to the transaction, including the lender. **IMPORTANT:** Cash on hand is not an acceptable source of donor gift funds.

VI. Property Related Acceptable Sources of Funds

a. Types of Personal Property

In order to obtain cash for closing, a borrower may sell various personal property items. The types of personal property items that a borrower can sell include: cars, recreational vehicles, stamps, coins, and baseball card collections.

b. Sale of Personal Property Documentation Requirement

If a borrower plans to sell personal property items to obtain funds for closing, he/she must provide:
• satisfactory estimate of the worth of the personal property items, and
• evidence that the items were sold.

The estimated worth of the items being sold may be in the form of:

- published value estimates issued by organizations, such as
    - automobile dealers, or
    - philatelic or numismatic associations, or

- a separate written appraisal by a qualified appraiser with no financial interest in the loan transaction.

Only the lesser of the estimated value or actual sales prices are considered as assets to close.

c. Net Sales Proceeds From a Property

The net proceeds from an arms-length sale of a currently owned property may be used for the cash investment on a new house. The borrower must provide a fully executed HUD-1 Settlement Statement as satisfactory evidence of the accrued cash sales proceeds.

If the property has not sold by the time of underwriting, condition loan approval by verifying the actual proceeds received by the borrower. The lender must document the:
- actual sale, and
- sufficiency of the net proceeds required for settlement.

Note: If the property has not sold by the time of the subject settlement, the existing mortgage must be included as a liability for qualifying purposes.

d. Commission From the Sale of the Property

If the borrower is a licensed real estate agent entitled to a real estate commission from the sale of the property being purchased, then he/she may use that amount for the cash investment, with no adjustment to the maximum mortgage required.

A family member entitled to the commission may also provide gift funds to the borrower.

e. Trade Equity

The borrower may agree to trade his/her real property to the seller as part of the cash investment. The amount of the borrower's equity contribution is determined by:
- using the lesser of the property's appraised value or sales price, and
- subtracting all liens against the property being traded, along with any real estate commission.

In order to establish the property value, the borrower must provide
- a residential appraisal no more than six months old to determine the property's value, and
- evidence of ownership.

Note: If the property being traded has an FHA-insured mortgage, assumption processing requirements and restrictions apply.

f. Rent Credit

The cumulative amount of rental payments that exceed the appraiser's estimate of fair market rent may be considered accumulation of the borrower's cash investment.

The following must be included in the endorsement package:

- rent with option to purchase agreement, and

- appraiser's estimate of market rent.

Conversely, treat the rent as an inducement to purchase with an appropriate reduction to the mortgage, if the sales agreement reveals that the borrower:

- has been living in the property rent-free, or
- has an agreement to occupy the property as a rental considerably below fair market value in anticipation of eventual purchase.

Exception: An exception may be granted when a builder:
- fails to deliver a property at an agreed to time, and
- permits the borrower to occupy an existing or other unit for less than market rent until construction is complete.

g. Sweat Equity Considered a Cash Equivalent

Labor performed, or materials furnished by the borrower before closing on the property being purchased (known as "sweat equity"), may be considered the equivalent of a cash investment, to the amount of the estimated cost of the work or materials.

VII. Loans and Grants as Acceptable Sources of Funds

a. Collateralized Loans

Funds may be borrowed for the total required investment, as long as satisfactory evidence is provided that the funds are fully secured by investment accounts or real property. These assets may include stocks, bonds, and real estate other than the property being purchased.

Certain types of loans secured against deposited funds, where repayment may be obtained through extinguishing the asset, do not require consideration of a repayment for qualifying purposes. The asset securing the loan may not be included as assets to close, or otherwise considered as available to the borrower. The types of deposited funds that can secure the loan include:

- signature loans

- the cash value of life insurance policies, or

- loans secured by 401(k) accounts.

b. Who Can Provide Collateralized Loans

An independent third party must provide the borrowed funds for collateralized loans.

The seller, real estate agent or broker, lender, or other interested party may not provide such funds.

Unacceptable borrowed funds include:
- unsecured signature loans
- cash advances on credit cards
- borrowing against household goods and furniture, and
- other similar unsecured financing.

c. Disaster Relief Grants and Loans

Grants or loans from state and Federal agencies, such as the Federal Emergency Management Agency (FEMA), that provide immediate housing assistance to individuals displaced due to a natural disaster, may be used for the borrower's cash investment.

Secured or unsecured disaster relief loans administered by the Small Business Association (SBA) may also be used. If the SBA loan will be secured against the property being purchased, it must be clearly subordinate to the FHA-insured mortgage.

Note: Any monthly payment arising from this type of loan must be included in the qualifying ratios.

VIII. Employer Programs as Acceptable Sources of Funds

a. Employer's Guarantee Plans

If the borrower's employer guarantees to purchase the borrower's previous residence as a result of relocation, he/she must submit evidence of the agreement.

The net proceeds must also be guaranteed.

b. Employer Assistance Plans

If the employer pays the following to attract or retain valuable employees, the payment is considered employee compensation:
- employee's closing costs
- any portion of the cash investment.
- mortgage insurance premiums, or

An adjustment to the maximum mortgage amount is not required.

If the employer provides this benefit after loan settlement, the borrower must provide evidence of sufficient cash for closing. **Note:** A salary advance cannot be considered as assets to close, since it represents an unsecured loan.

3. Borrower Secondary Financing

I. General Information on Secondary Financing

a. What Is Secondary Financing?

Any financing, other than an FHA-insured first mortgage, that creates a lien against the property is considered secondary financing. Such financing is not considered a gift, even if it is a "soft" or "silent" second or has other features forgiving the debt.

Note: A "soft" or "silent" second is secondary financing that has no monthly repayment provisions.

b. Secondary Financing Documentation Requirements

The lender must obtain from the provider of any secondary financing:
  - documentation showing the amount of funds provided to the borrower for each transaction, and
  - copies of the loan instruments for the endorsement binder.

Notes:
• FHA reserves the right to reject any secondary financing
  ▪ that does not serve the needs of the intended borrower, or
  ▪ where the costs to participants outweighs the benefits derived by the borrower.
• Costs incurred for participating in a down payment assistance secondary financing program may only be included in the amount of the second lien.

II. Permissible Borrower Secondary Financing

a. Financing From Government Agencies

FHA will insure a first mortgage loan on a property that has a second mortgage or lien by a Federal, State, or local government agency.

The monthly payments under the insured mortgage and second lien, plus housing expense and other recurring charges, cannot exceed the borrowers' ability to pay.

b. Financing From Nonprofit Organizations

With advance approval, FHA will insure a first mortgage loan on a property that has a second mortgage held by an approved nonprofit agency.

The monthly payments under the insured mortgage and second lien, plus housing expense and other recurring charges, cannot exceed the borrowers' ability to pay.

c. Financing From Private Individuals or Other Organizations

With advance approval, FHA will insure a first mortgage loan on a property that has a second mortgage or lien held by an individual or company, provided that:
- the secondary financing is disclosed at the time of application
- the required minimum cash investment is not financed
- the first and second mortgage together do not exceed FHA mortgage limits
- the borrower can afford the total amount of the payments
- any periodic payments are level and monthly
- there is no balloon payment during the first ten years, and
- there is no prepayment penalty.

d. Financing From Family Members

FHA permits family member lending on a secured or unsecured basis, up to 100 percent of the borrower's required funds to close. This lending may include the down payment, closing costs, prepaid expenses, and discount points.

If the money lent by the family member is secured against the subject property, whether borrowed from an acceptable source or from the family member's own savings, only the family member provider(s) may be the note holder. FHA will not approve any form of securitization of the note that results in any entity other than the family member being the note holder, whether at loan settlement or at any time during the mortgage life cycle.

e. Borrowing Policy for Borrowers 60 Years of Age and Older

With advance approval, borrowers 60 years of age and older may borrow the required funds to close for purchasing a principal residence under certain circumstances.

III. Government Agency Secondary Financing

a. Government Agencies That Can Provide Secondary Financing

Federal, state, local government, and nonprofit agencies considered instrumentalities of government may provide secondary financing for the borrower's entire amount of required funds to close.

b. Who Can Hold a Secondary Lien

When secondary financing is provided by a government agency, the secondary lien must be made or held by the eligible government body or instrumentality. Government units cannot use agents including nonprofit or for-profit enterprises to make the second lien, regardless of the source of funds. They can, however, be used to service the subordinate lien if regularly scheduled payments are made by the borrower. **Example:** Even if funds used for secondary financing funds are from an acceptable source, such as HUD HOME, a government unit, or an eligible nonprofit instrumentality, the subordinate lien must be in the name of the eligible entity: state, county, city, or eligible nonprofit instrumentality.

c. Policies for Loans Secured by Secondary Liens

Listed below are the policies for loans secured by secondary liens.

Financing Terms and Conditions

■ The FHA-insured first mortgage, when combined with any second mortgage or other junior lien from government agencies and nonprofit agencies considered instrumentalities of government, may not result in cash back to the borrower.

■ The FHA-insured first mortgage cannot exceed the FHA statutory limit for the area where the property is located. However, the combined indebtedness of the mortgages may exceed the FHA statutory limit.

■ The sum of all liens cannot exceed 100 percent of the cost to acquire the property. (Note: The cost to acquire the property is the sales price plus borrower-paid closing costs, discount points, repairs and rehabilitation expenses and prepaid expenses.)

■ The cost to acquire may exceed the appraised value of the property under these types of government assistance programs.

Required Monthly Payments

The required monthly payments, under both the FHA-insured first mortgage and the second mortgage or lien, plus other housing expenses and all recurring charges, cannot exceed the borrower's reasonable ability to pay.

Mortgage Application Disclosures

The source, amount, and repayment terms must be disclosed in the mortgage application, and the borrower must acknowledge that he/she understands and agrees to the terms.

IV. Nonprofit Agency Secondary Financing

a. Secondary Financing by a Nonprofit Agency Considered an Instrumentality of the Government

Nonprofit agencies may provide secondary financing provided that they are considered instrumentalities of the government.

Note: To be considered an instrumentality of the government, the nonprofit entity must be "established by a governmental body or with governmental approval or under special law to serve a particular public purpose or designated by law (statute or court opinion)."

b. FHA Requirement for Government Unit That Established the Nonprofit Entity

FHA requires that the unit of government that established the nonprofit must exercise either organizational control, operational control, or financial control of:

• the nonprofit agency in its entirety, or
• at a minimum, the specific borrower assistance program that is using FHA's credit enhancement.

c. HOC Responsibilities for Nonprofit Agency Approval

The appropriate HOC is responsible, based on information submitted by the nonprofit, for:
• approving the nonprofit agency
• determining if the agency can be considered an instrumentality of government, and
• reviewing applications from nonprofits that purport to be instrumentalities of government.

Note: The HOC is also responsible for approving nonprofit agencies that are not considered instrumentalities of government.

d. Secondary Financing by a Nonprofit Agency Not Considered an Instrumentality of the Government

Nonprofit agencies that are not considered instrumentalities of government may provide secondary financing provided that:

• the borrower makes a down payment of at least 3.5 percent of the lesser of the appraised value or the sales price of the property

• the combined amount of the first and second mortgages does not exceed the statutory loan limit for the area where the property is located, and

• the FHA-insured first mortgage, when combined with any second mortgage or junior lien from the nonprofit agency, may not result in cash back to the borrower.

V. Organizations and Individuals Providing Secondary Financing

a. Applicable LTV Ratio and Mortgage Limits

Other organizations or individuals may provide secondary financing when the combined amount of the first and second mortgages do not exceed the: applicable LTV ratio and maximum mortgage limit for the area.

b. Repayment Terms for Secondary Mortgages

Repayment terms for the second mortgage when borrowing from other organizations or private individuals must:
• not include a balloon payment before ten years (or other such term acceptable to FHA), unless the property is sold or refinanced, and

• permit repayment by the borrower, without penalty, after giving the lender 30 days advance notice.

c. Required Monthly Payment for Secondary Loans

The required monthly payment, under both the FHA-insured first mortgage and the second mortgage or lien, plus other housing expenses and all recurring charges, cannot exceed the borrower's reasonable ability to pay.

Any periodic payments due on the second mortgage must be calculated as an equal monthly payment.

VI. Family Member Secondary Financing

a. How a Family Member Can Help With Property Purchase

Family members may assist with the costs of acquiring a new home in the form of a loan.

Only the family member provider(s) may be the Note holder if the money lent is secured against the subject property.

FHA will not approve any form of securitization of the Note that results in any entity other than the family member being the noteholder, whether at loan settlement, or any time during the mortgage life cycle.

b. Amount Permitted on a Family Member Loan

FHA permits a family member to lend, on a secured or unsecured basis, a maximum of 100 percent of the borrower's required funds to close, including:
- down payment
- closing costs
- prepaid expenses, and
- discount points.

c. Restriction on a Borrower Being a Co- Obligor on the Note Securing a Borrowed Down Payment

When the funds loaned by the family member are borrowed from an acceptable source, the borrower may not be a co-obligor on the Note.

Example: A son or daughter in law may not be co-obligors on the Note used to secure the money borrowed by the parents that, in turn, was loaned to the borrower for the down payment on the property.

d. Additional Polices Regarding Financing Terms and Conditions

The table below describes additional policies regarding the various financing terms and conditions for loans secured with family member secondary financing.

Financing Category	Policy Description
Maximum insurable mortgage	The maximum insurable mortgage amount is not affected by loans from family members.

Combined financing amount	The combined amount of financing may not exceed 100 percent of
	
	• the lesser of the property's
	  ■ appraised value, or
	  ■ sales price, plus
	• the normal closing costs, prepaid expenses, and discount points.

Borrower cash back	While a family member may lend 100 percent of the borrower funds to close requirement, cash back to the borrower at closing (beyond the refund of any earnest money deposit) is not permitted.
Secondary financing payments	If periodic payments of the secondary financing are required, the combined payments may not exceed the borrower's reasonable ability to pay. **Note:** The secondary financing payments must be included in the total debt to income ratio (that is, the "back end" ratio) for qualifying purposes.
Second lien balloon payments	The second lien may not provide for a balloon payment within five years from the date of execution.
Family member supplying borrowed funds	If the family member providing the secondary financing borrows the funds, the lending source may not be an entity with an identity-of-interest in the sale of the property, such as: • the seller • a builder • the loan officer, or • the real estate agent. Mortgage companies that have retail banking affiliates may have that entity loan the funds to the family member. However, the terms and conditions for the loan that will be used for the secondary mortgage cannot be more favorable than it would be for other borrowers. **Example:** There may not be any special consideration given between the making of the mortgage, and the lending of funds to family members to be used for secondary financing for the purchase of the home.
Secondary financing document retention	An executed copy of the document describing the terms of the secondary financing must be maintained in the lender's file. An executed copy must also be provided in the endorsement binder.

VII. Secondary Financing for Borrowers 60 Years of Age and Older

a. Circumstances in Which an Older Borrower May Borrow the Cash Investment

Borrowers 60 years of age or older may borrow the required funds to close to purchase a principal residence when:

- the provider of secondary financing is
    - a relative
    - a close friend with a clearly defined interest in the borrower
    - the borrower's employer, or
    - an institution established for humanitarian or welfare purposes

- the provider of the secondary financing may not have an identity-of-interest in the sale of the property, such as with
    - a builder or seller, or
    - any person/organization associated with the builder or seller, and

- the principal amount of the insured mortgage loan, plus the Note or other evidence of indebtedness in connection with the property, does not exceed 100 percent of the value, plus prepaid expenses.

b. Note Interest Rate for Older Borrowers

The Note or other evidence of indebtedness may not bear an interest rate exceeding the interest rate of the insured mortgage.

CHAPTER SEVEN

Special Underwriting

1. Special Underwriting Instructions

I. FHA's TOTAL Mortgage Scorecard

a. Description of TOTAL

The acronym "TOTAL" stands for "Technology Open To Approved Lenders."

TOTAL Scorecard evaluates the overall creditworthiness of the applicants based on a number of credit variables and, when combined with the functionalities of the AUS, indicates a recommended level of underwriting and documentation to determine a loan's eligibility for insurance by the Federal Housing Administration (FHA).

b. Comparison of TOTAL to AUS

TOTAL is not an AUS. It is a scorecard that is used within an AUS.

To underwrite a loan electronically, a lender must process the request through an AUS that can communicate with TOTAL. TOTAL operates as a system-to-system connection to an AUS.

Together, TOTAL and the AUS either conclude that the borrowers' credit and capacity for repayment of the mortgage are acceptable or will refer the loan application to a Direct Endorsement (DE) underwriter for further consideration and review.

Regardless of the risk assessment provided by TOTAL, the lender remains accountable for compliance with FHA's eligibility requirements, as well as for any credit, capacity, and documentation requirements not covered in the FHA TOTAL Mortgage Scorecard User Guide.

Example: FHA will not be responsible for checking, through TOTAL, lender compliance with maximum mortgage amounts, computing debt-to-income ratios or other functions typically performed by an AUS. TOTAL provides only an assessment of the borrower's credit and capacity to repay.

c. TOTAL Scoring Recommendations

TOTAL will return recommendations of either:
- "Accept" or "Approve" (different AUSs use different wording), or
- "Refer."

The table below describes the TOTAL scoring recommendations.

TOTAL Recommendation	Description
Accept/Approve	This recommendation means that, based on the analysis of the credit and capacity to repay, the loan is eligible for FHA insurance provided that data entered into the AUS is true, complete, properly documented and accurate; and the documentation and other eligibility requirements are met.
Refer	This recommendation means that the lender must conduct a manual underwriting review, according to FHA requirements. The lender's DE underwriter must determine if the borrower is creditworthy in accordance with FHA standard credit policies and requirements.

Note: Per FHA policy, a borrower will not be denied an FHA mortgage solely on the basis of a risk assessment generated by TOTAL.

d. Rescoring and Tolerance Levels

TOTAL provides a risk assessment based on the specific data entered by lenders, such as terms and conditions of the loan, income and assets. Changes in those variables can result in a different risk assessment, and FHA requires that the loan be rescored using the new information.

However, where the differences are minor, rescoring is unlikely to trigger a different risk assessment. FHA therefore, provides a degree of tolerance before triggering a requirement for rescoring. The table below describes the tolerance level for rescoring requirements when assessing income and assets.

When assessing ...	There is no need to rescore if ...
cash reserves	the cash reserves verified are not more than 10 percent less than what the borrower reported on the loan application.
income	the verified income is not more than 5 percent less than what the borrower reported on the loan application.
tax and insurance escrows	the tax and insurance escrows used at scoring do not result in more than a 2 percentage point increase in the payment and debt-to-income ratios.

e. TOTAL User Guide

FHA has developed the TOTAL User Guide, which is a compilation of the specific credit policies and documentation requirements lenders must follow when using TOTAL.

The instructions in the Guide pertain only to those mortgage applications that had a TOTAL risk assessment, including those scored mortgages referred to an underwriter for manual underwriting.

II. Temporary Interest Rate Buydowns

a. Purpose of a Temporary Interest Rate Buydown

Interest rate buydowns are designed to reduce the borrower's monthly payment during the early years of the mortgage.

At settlement, an escrow account is established. Each month, the servicing lender draws down an amount equal to the difference in the principal and interest payment (P&I) at the Note rate, and the P&I at the buydown rate.

b. Eligible Transactions/ Mortgages

Temporary interest rate buydowns are permitted only on:
- purchase transactions, and
- fixed-rate mortgages.

c. Source of Buydown Funds

Buydown funds may come from:

- the seller
- the borrower
- the lender
- any other interested party

Funds from the seller or any other interested third party are considered seller contributions, and must be included in the 6 percent limit on seller contributions.

d. Underwriting Requirements for Qualifying the Borrower

While interest rate buydowns are permitted, the loan must be underwritten at the Note rate. Lenders may not underwrite at the buydown rate.

Buydowns may be treated only as a compensating factor.

e. Additional Interest Rate Buydown Instructions

Lender-funded buydowns on fixed-rate money mortgages through premium pricing are acceptable, provided that the funds do not result in a reduction greater than 2 percentage points below the Note rate.

f. Lender Responsibilities

Lenders are responsible for ensuring that:
- the buydown must not result in a reduction of more than two percentage points below the interest rate on the Note
- the buydown must not result in more than a one percentage point increase in the buydown rate.
- the borrower's payment may change only once a year
- the funds described in the escrow agreement are placed in escrow before or at closing
- a copy of the fully executed escrow agreement, signed by the borrower and provider of funds is provided in the mortgage case binder

Note: The underwriter may condition the loan approval for an executed buydown agreement at closing.

g. Escrow Agreement Requirements

The escrow agreement requirements with which all buydowns must comply are listed below:

- Any remaining escrow funds not distributed at the time the mortgage loan is prepaid must be applied to the outstanding balance due on the mortgage.

- In the event of foreclosure, the claim for mortgage insurance benefits must be reduced by the amount remaining in the buydown escrow account.

- The escrow agreement
  - may provide that assistance payments continue to buyers who assume the mortgage
  - must not permit reversion of undistributed escrow funds to the provider if the property is sold or the mortgage is prepaid in full, and
  - must not allow unexpended escrow funds to be provided to the borrower in cash, unless the borrower established the escrow account.

- Escrow funds must be held in an escrow account by a financial institution supervised by a Federal or state agency.

- Payments must be made by the escrow agent to the lender or servicing agent. If escrow payments are not received for any reason, the borrower is responsible for making the total payment as described in the mortgage note.

- FHA does not object to having the lender hold and administer the escrow funds, for up to 60 days, when there is an outstanding forward commitment to sell the mortgage.

Note: The escrow agreement text can also apply to repair escrows.

III. Construction Permanent Mortgage Program Eligibility

a. Construction Permanent Mortgage Features

A construction permanent mortgage loan:
- combines the features of
    - a construction loan, which is a short-term interim loan for financing the cost of construction, and
    - the traditional long-term permanent residential mortgage
- involves only one closing
- is considered a purchase transaction, for mortgage insurance and LTV purposes, and
- is made directly to an approved borrower by a lender.

b. Timing of Loan Closing and Insurance

On a construction permanent mortgage loan, there is only one closing, which is prior to the start of construction. At the closing, funds are disbursed to cover the purchase of the land and/or the manufactured housing unit. The balance of the mortgage proceeds are placed in an escrow account to be disbursed through draw requests until construction is completed.

Note: For CP on a manufactured home, there is a mandatory holdback of not less than ten percent for all cost components, excluding land.

Important: The loan is not insured until after construction is completed.

c. Criteria for Consideration as a Construction Permanent Mortgage

The table below describes the criteria for a loan to be considered a construction-permanent loan and eligible for FHA mortgage insurance.

Criteria	Description
Contract with the Builder	The borrower has contracted with a builder to construct the improvements. Note: This program is not available to a borrower acting as his/her own general contractor, unless the borrower is a licensed builder by profession. In this case, the acquisition cost must be determined by the actual documented cost to construct the improvements.
Lot Ownership	The borrower must own or be purchasing the lot at the closing of the CP loan. Note: If the contractor owns the lot, the lot must be included in the total contract price.
Lot Acquisition	If the borrower purchased the lot within the past six months, he/she must provide a copy of the HUD-1 Settlement Statement, or other settlement statement showing the acquisition cost. If the borrower owns the lot free-and-clear, the lender must document the date of ownership and omission or any liens from title work and settlement statements.

Verification of Loan Balance/ Escrow Account	The balance on the CP loan, when it is fully drawn, must be verified. The construction escrow account, if established, must be fully extinguished. Any remaining funds must be applied to the outstanding balance of the permanent loan.
Draw on Loan to Pay Off Lot	If the initial draw on the loan is for the purpose of paying off the lot, the borrower must provide a statement verifying the amount.
Sales Agreement	The borrower must provide a copy of the fully executed contract agreement, which includes the contractor's price to build.
Extras/Out-of-Pocket Costs	If the borrower is including extras over and above the contract specification and/or is paying out-of-pocket expense over and above the interim loan, then for all out-of-pocket construction costs the borrower must provide: • a breakdown of the extras • the cost of each • canceled checks, and/or • paid receipts.
Cash Back to Borrower	Replenishment of a borrower's own cash invested during construction is not considered cash back, provided the borrower can substantiate all out-of-pocket expenses used for construction with cancelled checks and/or paid receipts. Lenders must apply any excess funds from the construction proceeds to reduce the principal of the permanent loan. In general, the borrower is not to receive funds after closing. The borrower may receive up to $500 from any funds remaining after closing from unused prepaid expenses, which may include (but not limited to): • per diem interest to the end of the month on the new loan • hazard insurance premium deposits • monthly mortgage insurance premiums, and • any real estate tax deposits needed to establish the escrow accounts. **Note:** For manufactured homes that have been permanently erected on a site for less than one year prior to the date of the application for mortgage insurance, the borrower may not receive cash back at closing, even if the loan-to-value (LTV) is less than 85 percent.

IV. Construction Permanent Mortgage Program Requirements

a. Maximum Mortgage Amount

The maximum mortgage amount is determined by applying the LTV limits to the lesser of the appraised value or the acquisition cost.

The acquisition cost includes:
- the builder's price to build
- borrower-paid extras over and above the contract specification and/or out-of-pocket expenses over and above the interim loan
- cost of the land, and
- closing costs.

For extras over the contract specifications and out-of-pocket expenses, the borrower must provide:
- a breakdown of the extras
- the cost of each
- canceled checks, and/or
- paid receipts.

If the land has been owned more than six months, or was received as an acceptable gift, the value of the land may be used instead of its cost.

Note: If the value of the land is lower than acquisition cost, the value must be used in calculating the maximum mortgage amount.

Important: If the contractor for the improvements is also the seller of the land, the total acquisition cost for maximum mortgage purposes is the borrower's purchase price.

b. Equity in the Land as a Borrower's Down Payment

Equity in the land may be used for the borrower's down payment. However, if the advancement of the permanent loan results in the borrower receiving cash out in excess of $500, the maximum LTV is limited to 85 percent.

If the land has been owned more than six months, or was received as an acceptable gift, the value of the land may be used instead of its cost.

Note: If the value of the land is lower than acquisition cost, the value must be used in calculating the maximum mortgage amount.

Important: If the contractor for the improvements is also the seller of the land, the total acquisition cost for maximum mortgage purposes is the borrower's purchase price.

c. Permanent Loan Interest Rate

The permanent mortgage loan interest rate is established at closing. However, a lender may offer a "ceiling/floor" where the borrower may "float" the interest rate during construction.

At the point of interest rate lock-in, the agreement between the lender and the borrower must provide that the permanent mortgage will not exceed a specific maximum interest rate, and that, depending on market fluctuations, the borrower will be allowed to lock-in a lower rate.

The borrower must qualify for the mortgage at the maximum rate at which the permanent mortgage may be set.

d. Timeframe for Start of Amortization

Amortization must begin no later than the first of the month, following 60 days from the date of
- final inspection, or
- issuance of certificate of occupancy, whichever is later.

e. Disclosure to the Borrower on Eligibility for Insurance

The lender must provide a disclosure to the borrower explaining: that the loan is not eligible for FHA mortgage insurance until after a final inspection or issuance of a certificate of occupancy by the local governmental jurisdiction, whichever is later and that FHA has no obligation until the mortgage is endorsed for issuance.

f. Draw on Loan to Payoff Lot

If the initial draw on the loan was for the purpose of paying off the lot or land, the borrower must provide a statement verifying the payoff amount.

g. Remitting UFMIP

FHA must receive the UFMIP within 10 calendar days of closing

h. Construction Period Fees

Unless a separate agreement is made specifying responsibility, the following costs are paid by the builder during construction:

- construction loan interest
- title update charges
- other financing charges
- commitment fees
- real estate taxes
- inspection fees
- hazard insurance

i. Disbursing Funds

It is the lender's responsibility on a construction permanent mortgage loan to obtain written approval from the borrower before each draw payment is provided to the builder.

j. Request for Endorsement

The lender must submit a request for endorsement within 60 days of the final inspection or issuance of certificate of occupancy, whichever is later. **Note:** During construction, the loan is not FHA-insured.

k. Use of Warehouse Lines- of- Credit for Construction Permanent Loans on Manufactured Homes

Lenders may use warehouse lines-of-credit for manufactured homes when the construction, installation and/or alternative construction, from start to completion, can be accomplished in 30 to 60 calendar days. Lenders may also utilize alternative arrangements to fund both closing and construction period disbursements, such as non-traditional warehouse lines, business lines-of-credit, or other available sources of interim capital.

Borrowers are not to be charged or otherwise held responsible for the costs associated with interim financing, unless they have executed a separate agreement acknowledging their responsibility for such costs. These costs may not result in an increase in the amount of the permanent loan and/or the monthly principal and interest payment at the time any modification to the note is made.

V. Construction Permanent Mortgage Documentation Requirements for Closing and Endorsement

a. Documentation Requirements for Closing

Standard FHA documents are used when closing a construction-permanent mortgage loan, with the addition of a: Construction Rider or Allonge to the Note and Construction Loan Agreement.

These construction documents may be in any form acceptable to the lender, but they must provide that all special construction terms end when the construction loan converts to a permanent loan.

The Construction Loan Agreement must outline:
- the terms and conditions of the construction loan, and
- its conversion to a permanent loan.

After conversion, only the permanent loan terms continue to be effective, making the permanent loan eligible for FHA mortgage insurance.

Lenders must also provide an executed Loan Modification Agreement to confirm the existence of a permanent loan and that the corresponding amortizing interest rate on the mortgage loan shall commence or commenced within 60 days of the property being 100% complete.

b. Documentation Required for Endorsement

Prior to endorsement, the lender must obtain:

- a certification, signed by the borrower after conversion to the permanent loan, that the mortgaged property is free and clear of all liens other than the mortgage

- verification that the construction loan has been fully drawn down

- copies of canceled checks and paid receipts for all the borrower's out-of-pocket construction costs, and

- all property-related requirements for new construction.

c. Making Changes to the Note for the Permanent Loan

The lender must provide acceptable modification instruments that modify the note and security instrument (as applicable), if there are changes made to the Note, such as a:
- reduction in the
  - monthly payment amount,
  - interest rate, or
  - principal balance resulting from the application of excess funds, or
- change in first payment date.

d. Application of Gift Funds when Closing a Construction Permanent Loan

Gifts from eligible sources for down payment shall be applied to the permanent financing on the HUD-1 Settlement Statement at the time of closing, and not to interim financing for the borrower, in order to receive full benefit of the credit for the CP transaction. For a refinance transaction, the gift funds can only be applied once, to either the construction loan or the permanent loan.

VI. Mortgage Insurance for Disaster Victims

a. Description of the Section 203(h) Program

Under the Section 203(h), Mortgage Insurance for Disaster Victims program, FHA provides mortgage insurance to assist victims of Presidentially-declared disasters. This program goes into effect when the President declares the disaster, and remains in effect for one year from the date of declaration.

The Federal Emergency Management Agency (FEMA) provides listings of specific affected counties and cities, and corresponding disaster declaration dates. **Note:** The FEMA information can be found at http://www.fema.gov/disasters.

b. Required Borrower Evidence of Residence and Destruction

Under Section 203(h), the borrower's previous residence must have been in the disaster area and must have been destroyed or damaged to such an extent that reconstruction or replacement is necessary. Borrowers must provide conclusive evidence of this fact, as outlined in the table below.

Note: The borrower may have been the owner of the property or a renter of the property affected.

Conclusive evidence of ...	Includes ...
a permanent residence in the affected area	• a valid driver's license • a voter registration card, or • utility bills.
destruction of the residence	• an insurance report • an inspection report by an independent fee inspector or government agency, or • conclusive photographic evidence showing the destruction or damage.

c. Eligible Properties

The following properties are eligible under the Section 203(h) program:
- one unit detached homes
- units in an approved condominium project, or
- "spot loan" in condominiums.

Two, three, and four unit properties may not be purchased under the program.

d. Amount of Financing for Eligible Borrowers

An eligible borrower may receive 100 percent financing of the sales price and no down payment is required. However, closing costs and prepaid expenses not paid by the seller must be
- paid by the borrower in cash, or
- paid through premium pricing.

Note: Adjustable Rate Mortgages (ARMs) may be used with the Section 203(h) program.

e. Section 203(h) Maximum Mortgage Amounts

Maximum mortgage amounts for the Section 203(h) program are the same as for the Section 203(b) program. The list can be accessed from the lender's Web page on HUD's Web site at www.hud.gov or on the FHA Connection.

f. Timeframe for Submission of Loan Application

The borrower's mortgage loan application must be submitted to the lender within one year of the President's declaration of the disaster.

g. Using Section 203(k) With 203(h) for Rehabilitation Mortgages

The requirement to complete a dwelling more than one year preceding the date of the mortgage insurance application under the Section 203(k), Rehabilitation Home Mortgage Insurance program, does not apply to properties in a disaster area.

Damaged residences are eligible for Section 203(k) mortgage insurance, regardless of the age of the property. The residence needs only to have been completed and ready for occupancy for eligibility under Section 203(k).

Homes that have been demolished, or will be razed as part of the rehabilitation work, are eligible, provided the existing foundation system is not affected, and will remain in place and be used. The complete foundation system must remain in place.

h. Section 203(k) Financing Percentages

The type of mortgage being made determines the percentage of financing when using Section 203(k) with 203(h) for rehabilitation mortgages. In other words, normal LTV ratios apply to Section 203(k) mortgages made in disaster areas.

i. Section 203(h) Underwriting Guidance

Since many borrowers affected by a major disaster will experience difficulty in providing traditional documentation regarding employment and funds for closing due to the disaster, lenders should be as flexible as prudent decision making permits, when applying FHA's underwriting criteria and documentation requirements.

To the extent possible, lenders should be accommodating towards borrowers:

- eligible for Section 203(h) mortgages, whether or not they opt for another FHA program, such as 203(k), regarding gaps in
  - employment
  - documentation for employment
  - available funds, and
  - qualifying ratios, and

- when evaluating the following that were the direct result of a disaster, as reported into HUD's Credit Alert Interactive Voice Response System (CAIVRS):
  - recent derogatory credit
  - bankruptcy
  - foreclosure
  - deed-in-lieu of foreclosure, and
  - delinquent federal obligations.

j. Section 203(h) Example Scenarios and General Underwriting Guidance

The table that follows contains:
- example scenarios involving disaster victims, and
- guidelines for using alternative documentation when traditional documentation is unavailable.

Note: The guidelines below are meant to provide general guidance only and do not address all of the circumstances in which alternative documentation can be used. Each case is different, and ultimately needs to be evaluated on its own merits.

Underwriting Category	Guideline
Credit	Lenders should be able to determine if derogatory credit occurred subsequent to a disaster. If the credit report indicates satisfactory credit prior to a disaster, and any derogatory credit subsequent to the date of the disaster can be related to the effects of the disaster, FHA will consider that the borrower is a satisfactory credit risk, for the underwriting standards.
CAIVRS	FHA determines that a borrower is not eligible for FHA insurance if CAIVRS indicates the borrower is presently delinquent, or has had a claim paid within the previous three years on a loan made or insured by HUD on his/her behalf. FHA is adding, to the list of exceptions to this rule, situations involving Presidentially-declared disasters. If the borrower is reported in CAIVRS, but the credit report indicates the loan was current prior to the disaster, and any delinquency or claim paid can be related to the effects of the disaster, the borrower may be considered eligible. As with any CAIVRS authorization, lenders may contact the appropriate HOC for additional Section 203(h) underwriting information and guidance.

Income	Borrower's affected by a disaster may not be able to document past or present employment. If prior employment cannot be verified because records are destroyed, and he/she has a current position in the same or similar field, it may still be possible to consider the income. W-2s and tax returns may be obtained from the IRS to confirm prior employment and income. If this information cannot be obtained on a timely basis, the credit report may indicate the borrower's prior employment. Lenders can consider short-term employment, due to the disaster. It is anticipated that lenders will make every effort to obtain documentation about prior employment, and FHA will be flexible on the documentation requirements. Note: Lenders should document the efforts taken to obtain traditional documentation.

Qualifying Ratios	When a borrower is purchasing a new home, yet still has an outstanding mortgage on a property located in a FEMA Disaster Area, the lender may exclude the mortgage payment on the previous residence from the qualifying ratio calculation, if the borrower provides the lender with information indicating that
	
	  • he/she is working with the servicing lender to appropriately address his/her mortgage obligation, and
	  • any property insurance proceeds will be applied to the mortgage on the damaged home.

Assets	Lenders should encourage a borrower to access his/her financial institution's Web sites to attempt to download statements confirming assets needed to close the loan, if hard copy bank records are unavailable. Lenders should document the efforts to verify assets, and make every effort to ensure that the borrower will have funds to complete the transaction.
Liabilities	When a borrower has a continued mortgage obligation on a prior loan securing a property that has been destroyed or damaged, FHA understands that the record may show late payments as a result of a disaster. Lenders should not consider the outstanding mortgage obligation on destroyed, or seriously damaged properties when determining a borrower's ability to make payments on a new loan, provided the requirements under Qualifying Ratios in this table have been met. FHA takes the position that insurance settlements are likely to pay-off remaining obligations. However, if a borrower was three or more months delinquent on his/her loan prior to the disaster, and the property is destroyed, it would not be prudent for a lender to make a new loan unless he/she can show and document extenuating circumstances.

VII. Energy Efficient Homes

a. EEH Qualifying Ratios

For a mortgage loan involving an energy efficient home (EEH), the two benchmark qualifying ratios may be exceeded by up to 2 percentage points when the borrower is purchasing or refinancing an EEH.

These higher housing expense- and obligations-to-income ratios are justified due to the anticipated energy costs savings, and become 33 percent and 45 percent, respectively.

b. Eligible EEH Properties

All properties meeting the 2000 International Energy Conservation Code (IECC), formerly known as the Model Energy code (MEC) are considered:
- energy efficient, and
- eligible for the 2 percentage points increase in the EEH qualifying ratios.

Note: Both new and existing one- to four-unit properties are eligible, including one-unit condominiums and manufactured housing.

c. EEH General Underwriting Policy

An EEH mortgage is initially underwritten as if the energy package did not exist, that is, by using standard FHA underwriting standards, qualifying income ratios, and maximum mortgage/minimum down payment requirements without regard to the energy package.

For an EEH mortgage on new construction, as well as those homes that were built to the 2000 IECC, or are being retrofitted to that standard, the borrower can obtain "stretch ratios" of 33 percent and 45 percent, in addition to the cost of the improvements.

d. EEH General Underwriting Procedures

Once it is determined that both the borrower and the property qualify for an FHA-insured mortgage, the lender must determine the dollar amount of the cost-effective energy package that may be added to the loan amount, using the energy rating report and EEM worksheet.

This dollar amount cannot exceed 5 percent (not to exceed $8,000) of the property's value, or $4,000, whichever is greater. Regardless of the property's value, every borrower who otherwise qualifies can finance at least $4,000 of the costs of the Energy Package, if the cost exceeds $4,000.

The calculated amount must be added to the approved base loan amount to total the final FHA-insured loan amount, before adding any upfront mortgage insurance premium (UFMIP).

The FHA maximum loan limit for the area may be exceeded by the cost of the energy efficient improvements.

e. EEH Underwriting Procedures for New Construction Mortgages

When qualifying the borrower, the cost of the energy package must be subtracted from the sales price, since the builder has included the improvements in the sales price.

Calculate the qualifying ratios on the lower amount.

f. EEH Policy Guidance for Streamline Refinances

The borrower's principal and interest (P&I) payment on the new loan including the energy package, may be greater than the P&I payment on the current loan, provided that the estimated monthly energy savings as shown on the Home Energy Rating Systems (HERS) report exceeds the increase in the P&I.

VIII. Restriction on Advanced Mortgage Payments

a. Advanced Mortgage Payment Requirements

FHA does not permit a lender to collect from the borrower advance payment(s) of the mortgage, as a condition for making a FHA-insured mortgage.

Lenders are not permitted to require a borrower to make mortgage payments to the lender in advance of the borrower's mortgage payment requirements under the security instruments, either through the use of:
  • post-dated checks
  • cash, or
  • any other form of payment.

IX. Condominium Units Utility Expenses

a. Condominium Utility Expenses

The portion of a condominium fee that is clearly attributable to utilities may be subtracted from the Homeowners Association (HOA) dues, before computing ratios, provided the borrower provides proper documentation, such as documentation from the utility company.

X. HUD Real Estate Owned (REO) Acquisitions

a. Calculating Loans on HUD REO Sales With Repair Escrow

On a HUD Real Estate Owned (REO) property that requires no more than $5,000 for repairs to meet FHA's property requirements, 110 percent of the estimated cost of the repairs may be included in the mortgage amount.

2. Adjustable Rate Mortgages (ARMs)

a. Terms and Definitions Related to ARMs:

• **adjusted interest rate**	The adjusted interest rate is the new interest rate effective for the 12-month period following each Change Date. The Adjusted Interest Rate becomes the Existing Interest Rate on the next Change Date.
• **calculated interest rate**	The calculated interest rate is the Current Index, plus the Margin, rounded to the nearest one-eighth of one percentage point (0.125%). The Calculated Interest Rate is used to determine the Adjusted Interest Rate
• **change date**	The change date is the effective date of an adjustment to the interest rate
• **current index**	The current index is the most recently available Index published 30 calendar days before the Change Date.
• **existing interest rate**	The existing interest rate is the interest rate effective immediately prior to any adjustment on the pending Change Date.
• **initial interest rate**	The Initial Interest Rate is the rate stated in the ARM Note that will be in effect from the date of the first monthly payment for the ARM.
• **index**	Index is the weekly average yield on United States Treasury securities adjusted to a constant maturity of one year
• **margin**	Margin is the agreed upon number of percentage points added to the Current Index for determining the Calculated Interest Rate.

I. General Information on ARMs

a. ARM Interest Rate Adjustments and Caps

The table below describes the annual interest rate adjustment and interest rate cap over the life of the five types of ARM loans.

When the ARM is for ...	Then the annual interest rate adjustment, after the initial fixed interest rate period, is ...	And the interest rate cap over the life of the loan is ...

• one-year • three years, or • five years	one percentage point	five percentage points.
• five years • seven years, or • ten years	two percentage point	six percentage points

Note: FHA added the two options for the five year ARM in order to meet the needs of homebuyers, lenders and the secondary mortgage market.

b. Hybrid ARM Eligibility

Owner-occupied principal residences being insured under the following programs are eligible for hybrid ARMs:
- Section 203(b), Home Mortgage Insurance Program
- Section 203(h), Home Mortgage Insurance for Disaster Victims Program
- 203(k), Rehabilitation Home Mortgage Insurance Program, and
- 234(c), Mortgage Insurance for Condominium Units.

Nonprofits, including organizations normally eligible as borrowers, and government agencies are not permitted to apply for the hybrid ARM products.

c. Maximum Number of ARM Units

The aggregate number of all ARMs insured by FHA in any fiscal year may not exceed 30 percent of the aggregate number of mortgages insured during the preceding fiscal year.

FHA will notify lenders when the maximum percentage is close to being reached during any fiscal year.

II. ARM Underwriting Requirements

a. ARM Processing and Underwriting Requirement

ARM loans must be processed and underwritten using the initial interest rate negotiated between the lender and borrower as stated on Form HUD 92900-A, Addendum to Uniform Residential Loan Application.

Mortgage credit processing must be in accordance with existing FHA instructions, except as modified subsequently in this topic.

b. ARM Pre Loan Disclosure

At the time of the loan application, the lender must provide the borrower with a written explanation of the:

- nature of the proposed obligation, and
- features of an ARM, consistent with the disclosure requirements applicable to variable-rate mortgages secured by a principal dwelling under the Truth-in-Lending Act (TILA), "Regulation Z" at:

  - 15 United States Code (USC) 1601, and

  - 12 Code of Federal Regulations (CFR) 226.18 .

Additionally, the lender must provide the borrower with a hypothetical monthly payment schedule that displays the maximum potential increases in monthly payments for the term of the ARM. The hypothetical payment schedule should illustrate the maximum increases over the shortest possible time frame.

Example: A seven year ARM payment schedule would show the maximum potential increases over the three years following the initial fixed interest rate period of seven years.

Notes: FHA relies on lenders to comply with TILA, and does not provide disclosures for the ARM products.

The ARM disclosure statement, signed by all borrowers, must accompany the loan application, and applicable FHA addenda.

c. Basis for Annual MIP

The mortgage insurance premium (MIP) amount and any termination provisions must be based on the initial interest rate throughout the term of the loan, regardless of the annual interest rate adjustments to the loan.

d. Interest Rate Information

The following rate information must be specified on the mortgage documents: initial interest rate, margin, frequency of adjustments, and date of the first adjustment to the interest rate

e. Borrower Qualifying on the 1 Year ARM

Borrowers choosing the 1 year ARM must qualify for payments based on the contract or initial rate plus one percentage point. This only applies to the 1 year ARM where the loan-to-value (LTV) is 95 percent or greater.

For this purpose, the LTV is defined as the lesser of:

- the base loan amount divided by the appraiser's estimate of value, or
- the percentage shown on the "LTV" line under the Qualifying Ratios section on the HUD-92900-LT.

f. Borrower Qualifying on the 3, 5, 7, or 10 Year ARM

Borrower's choosing the three, five, seven, or ten year ARMs should be qualified at the entry level or Note rate. These ARMs do not require underwriting at the one percentage point above the Note.

g. Temporary Interest Rate Buydowns

Any form of temporary interest rate buydown is prohibited for all ARMs, regardless of LTV. If there is a permanent buydown, underwriting must be based on the rate in the application.

h. ARM Loan Maturity

ARM loan maturities shall not exceed 30 years.

i. Model ARM and Note

Mortgage lenders must modify the model ARM Note form to accommodate the type of ARM being offered, including the: Change Date, limits on the interest rate changes associated with the initial fixed rate period of the ARM, and lifetime caps.

j. Amortization Provisions

The ARM must: be fully-amortizing and contain amortization provisions that allow for periodic adjustments in the rate of interest charged.

3. Streamline Refinances

I. Requirements for Streamline Refinances

a. Description of a Streamline Refinance

Streamline refinances: are designed to lower the monthly principal and interest payments on a current FHA-insured mortgage, and must involve no cash back to the borrower, except for minor adjustments at closing that are not to exceed $500.

b. Permissible Geographic Areas for Streamline Refinances

Lenders may solicit and process streamline refinance applications from any area of the country, provided the lender is approved for Direct Endorsement (DE) by at least one Homeownership Center (HOC).

c. Use of Appraisals on Streamline Refinances

FHA does not require an appraisal on a streamline refinance. These transactions can be made with or without an appraisal.

FHA does not require repairs to be completed on streamline refinances with appraisals, with the exception of lead-based paint repairs. However, the lender may require completion of repairs as a condition of the loan.

d. Ignoring or Setting Aside an Appraisal on Streamline Refinances

If an appraisal has been performed on a property, and the appraised value is such that the borrower would be better advised to proceed as if no appraisal had been made, then
> • the appraisal may be ignored and not used, and
> • a notation of this decision must be made on the HUD-92900-LT, FHA Loan Underwriting and Transmittal Summary.

e. Reviewing HUD LDP and GSA Exclusion Lists

HUD's CAIVRS does not need to be checked for streamline refinances, but the following must still be reviewed for all borrowers:
> • HUD Limited Denial of Participation (LDP) List, and
> • General Services Administration (GSA) List of Parties Excluded from Federal Procurement or Non-procurement Programs.

f. Credit Report Requirements and Availability of Credit Score for Streamline Refinances

FHA does not require a credit report, except for credit qualifying streamline refinances. However, the lender may require this as part of their credit policy.

If a credit score is available, the lender must enter the credit score into FHA Connection (FHAC). If more than one credit score is available, the lender must enter all available credit scores into FHAC.

g. Underwriting Requirements, Use of TOTAL Scorecard and Loan Application Documentation

Lenders may not use the TOTAL Scorecard on streamline refinance transactions. If a lender uses TOTAL to underwrite a loan, that loan must be underwritten and closed as a rate and term (no cash-out) refinance transaction.

Lenders may no longer use an abbreviated version of the Uniform Residential Loan Application (URLA).

Due to various disclosure requirements, the application for mortgage insurance must be signed and dated by the borrower(s) before the loan is underwritten. Lenders are permitted to process and underwrite the loan after the borrower(s) and interviewer complete the initial URLA and initial form HUD 92900A, HUD/VA Addendum to Uniform Residential Loan Application.

The lender must continue to ensure compliance with the Equal Credit Opportunity Act (ECOA) and all other regulatory requirements.

h. Certification of Borrower's Employment and Income for a Streamline Refinance and Required Case Binder Documentation

The lender must certify that the borrower was employed and had income at the time of loan application.

The lender certification must be:
- in writing
- on company letterhead, and
- signed and dated.

When submitting the loan for insurance endorsement, the lender must include the signed certification and a copy of the payoff statement in the case binder.

Note: Certification requirements are set forth in Title 18 U.S.C 1014, which provides in part that whoever knowingly and willfully makes or uses a document containing any false, fictitious, or fraudulent statement or entry, in any matter in the jurisdiction of any department or agency of the United States, shall be fined not more than $1,000,000 or imprisoned for not more than 30 years or both, and violation of this or others may result in debarment and civil liability for damages suffered by HUD.

II. Credit Qualifying Streamline Refinances

a. Features of a Credit Qualifying Streamline Refinance

Credit qualifying streamline refinances contain all the normal features of a streamline refinance, but provide a level of assurance for continued performance on the mortgage.

The lender must provide evidence that the remaining borrowers have an acceptable credit history and ability to make payments.

b. Lender Responsibility for Credit Documentation and Borrower Qualifying

For credit qualifying streamline refinancing, the lender must:
- verify the borrower's income and credit report
- compute the debt-to-income ratios, and
- determine that the borrower will continue to make mortgage payments.

c. Required Usage of a Credit Qualifying Streamline Refinance

Credit qualifying streamline refinances must be considered:

- when a change in the mortgage term will result in an increase in the mortgage payment more than 20 percent

- when deletion of a borrower or borrowers will trigger the due-on-sale clause

- following the assumption of a mortgage that
  - occurred less than six months previously, and
  - does not contain restrictions (that is, the due-on-sale clause) limiting assumptions only to creditworthy borrowers, and

- following an assumption of a mortgage that
  - occurred less than six months previously, and
  - did not trigger the transferability restriction (that is, the due-on-sale clause), such as in a property transfer resulting from a divorce decree or by devise or descent.

Note: The use of a credit qualifying streamline refinance in situations in which the change in mortgage term will result in an increase in the mortgage payment is only permissible for:

- owner-occupied principal residences

- secondary residences meeting the requirements, and

- those investment properties purchased by governmental agencies and eligible nonprofit organizations

III. Streamline Refinance Borrower and Property Related Requirements

a. Borrower Cash to Close on a Streamline Refinance

If assets are needed to close, the lender must verify, document, and determine the acceptability of the assets to be utilized.

b. Holding Period Prior to Borrower Eligibility on a Streamline Refinance

A borrower is eligible for a streamline refinance without credit qualifying if
- he/she has owned the property for at least six months, and
- the previous borrowers received a release of liability at the time of the assumption.

This rule applies to mortgages that do not contain restrictions limiting the assumption only to credit worthy assumptors.

Note: Typically these types of mortgages were made prior to December 1989.

c. Borrower Additions or Deletions to the Title

Individuals may be added to the title on a streamline refinance without: a credit worthiness review and triggering the due-on-sale clause.

Individuals may be deleted from the title on a streamline refinance, only when:

- an assumption of a mortgage not containing a due-on-sale clause occurred more than six months previously, and

- the assumptor can document that he/she has made the mortgage payments during this interim period, or

• following an assumption of a mortgage in which:

- the transferability restriction (due-on-sale clause) was not triggered, such as in a property transfer resulting from a divorce decree or by devise or descent

- the assumption or quit-claim of interest occurred more than six months previously, and

- the remaining owner-occupant can demonstrate that he/she has made the mortgage payments during this time.

d. Withdrawn Condominium Approvals

If approval of a condominium project has been withdrawn, FHA will insure only streamline refinances without appraisals for that condominium project.

e. Seven Unit Exemptions

An eligible investor that has a financial interest in more than seven rental units, may only refinance without appraisals.

f. Seasoning and Mortgage Payment History Requirement for Borrower Eligibility on a Streamline Refinance

At the time of loan application, the borrower must:

• have made at least six payments on the FHA-insured mortgage being refinanced, and

• exhibit an acceptable payment history as described in the table below.

If the mortgage has ...	Then the borrower...
less than 12 months payment history	must have made all mortgage payments within the month due
12 months payment history or greater	must have • experienced no more than one 30 day late payment in the preceding 12 months, and • made all mortgage payments within the month due for the three months prior to the date of the loan application.

IV. Types of Permissible Streamline Refinances

a. No Cost Refinances

No cost refinances, in which the lender charges a premium interest rate to defray the borrower's closing costs and/or prepaid items, are permitted.

The lender may also offer an interest free advance of amounts equal to the present escrow balances on the existing mortgage to establish a new escrow account.

b. Transactions Ineligible for Streamline Refinance Term Reduction

A transaction for the purpose of reducing the mortgage term, must be underwritten and closed as a rate and term (no cash-out) refinance transaction.

c. Ineligibility of Delinquent Mortgages

Delinquent mortgages are not eligible for streamline refinancing until the loan is brought current.

d. ARM to ARM Refinancing

An ARM may be refinanced to another ARM, provided that there is a net tangible benefit to the borrower. ARM to ARM refinances may be transacted with or without an appraisal. **Important:** An ARM may be used only for refinancing principal residences.

e. ARM to Fixed Rate Refinancing

The interest rate on the new fixed rate mortgage will be no greater than 2 percentage points above the current rate of the one-year ARM. For hybrid ARMs, the total mortgage payment on the new fixed rate mortgage may not increase by more than 20 percent.

Example: Total mortgage payment on the hybrid ARM is $895; the total mortgage payment for the new fixed rate mortgage must be $1,074 or less.

f. Fixed Rate to ARM Refinancing

A fixed rate mortgage may be refinanced to a one year ARM, with or without an appraisal, provided that the interest rate of the new mortgage is at least two percentage points below the interest rate of the current mortgage.

g. GPM to Fixed Rate Refinancing

A section 245 Graduated Payment Mortgage (GPM) may be refinanced to a fixed rate mortgage, with or without an appraisal, provided that there is a net tangible benefit to the borrower.

If the streamline refinance is completed without an appraisal, the new mortgage amount may exceed the statutory limit by the accrued negative amortization, and the new UFMIP.

h. GPM to ARM Refinancing

A GPM may be refinanced to an ARM, provided that the note rate results in a reduction to the current principal and interest payments.

If the streamline refinance is completed without an appraisal, the new mortgage amount may exceed the statutory limit by the accrued negative amortization, and the new UFMIP.

i. Section 203(k) to Section 203(b) Refinancing

A section 203(k) rehabilitation mortgage may be refinanced into a Section 203(b) mortgage after all work is complete. The rehabilitation work is considered complete by:

- a fully executed certificate of completion
- closing the rehabilitation escrow account with a final release, and
- the lender entering the required close out information into the FHA Connection, or its functional equivalent.

Note: Before lenders can order a case number for a refinance of a Section 203(k) mortgage, the previous lender must have completed the Section 203(k) closeout process in FHA Connection.

j. Section 235 to Section 203(b) Refinancing

Lenders may refinance Section 235 mortgages to Section 203(b) mortgages using streamline underwriting procedures.

Any overpaid subsidy that has been paid by the lender to HUD, and is part of the borrower's mortgage account, can be included in the Section 203(b) mortgage amount, provided that the mortgage amount does not exceed the maximum mortgage permitted under the streamline refinancing requirements.

If HUD has a junior lien that was part of the original Section 235 financing, HUD will subordinate the junior lien to the Section 203(b) mortgage that refinances the Section 235 mortgage.

k. Investment Properties or Secondary Residences Ineligible for Streamline Refinance

In addition to meeting the requirement for a reduction in the total mortgage payment, investment properties or secondary residences are not eligible for streamline refinancing to ARMs.

V. Establishing Net Tangible Benefit of Streamline Refinance

a. Definition of Net Tangible Benefit of Streamline Refinance

The lender must determine that there is a net tangible benefit as a result of the streamline refinance transaction, with or without an appraisal.

Net tangible benefit is defined as a:

- reduction in the total mortgage payment, which includes
  - principal
  - interest
  - taxes and insurances
  - homeowners' association fees
  - ground rents
  - special assessments, and
  - all subordinate liens, or
- refinance from an ARM to a fixed rate mortgage.

b. Net Tangible Benefit of Reduction in Total Mortgage Payment from Streamline Refinance

To qualify as a net tangible benefit, the new total mortgage payment must be at least five percent lower than the total mortgage payment for the mortgage being refinanced.

Example: Total mortgage payment on the existing FHA-insured mortgage is $895; the total mortgage payment for the new FHA-insured mortgage must be $850 or less.

Note: This requirement applies when refinancing from:

• fixed rate to fixed rate	• ARM to ARM	• GPM to fixed rate
• GPM to ARM	• 203(k) to 203(b)	• 235 to 203(b)

c. Net Tangible Benefit of ARM to Fixed Rate Refinance

The interest rate on the new fixed rate mortgage will be no greater than two percentage points above the current rate of a one-year ARM.

Important: For hybrid ARMs, the total mortgage payment on the new fixed rate mortgage may not increase by more than 20 percent. **Example:** Total mortgage payment on the hybrid ARM is $895; the total mortgage payment for the new fixed rate mortgage must be $1,074 or less.

d. Net Tangible Benefit of Fixed Rate to ARM Refinance

Fixed rate mortgages may be refinanced to one-year ARMs provided that the interest rate in the new mortgage is at least two percentage points below the interest rate of the current mortgage.

CHAPTER EIGHT

Property Valuation & Appraisals

I. General Information on Property Valuation and Eligibility

a. Purpose of Property Valuation

The purpose of the property valuation process is to: determine eligibility for mortgage insurance based on the condition and location of a property and estimate the value of the property for mortgage insurance purposes. The appraisal is the lender's tool for making this determination.

b. Lender Responsibility for Appraisers

The lender is equally responsible, along with the appraiser, for the quality, integrity, accuracy and thoroughness of the appraisal. The lender will be held accountable by HUD if the lender knew, or should have known, that there were problems with the integrity, accuracy and thoroughness of an appraisal submitted to FHA for mortgage insurance purposes. Lenders that submit appraisals to HUD that do not meet FHA requirements are subject to the imposition of sanctions by the HUD Mortgagee Review Board.

Note: This applies to both sponsor lenders that underwrite loans and loan correspondent lenders that originate loans on behalf of their sponsors.

c. Appraisal and Appraisal Management Company (AMC)/Third Party Organization Fees

FHA does not require the use of AMCs or other third party organizations for appraisal ordering, but recognizes that some lenders use AMCs and/or other third party organizations to help ensure appraiser independence.

FHA-approved lenders must ensure that:

> • FHA Appraisers are not prohibited by the lender, AMC or other third party, from recording the fee the appraiser was paid for the performance of the appraisal in the appraisal report

- FHA Roster appraisers are compensated at a rate that is customary and reasonable for appraisal services performed in the market area of the property being appraised

- the fee for the actual completion of an FHA appraisal may not include a fee for management of the appraisal process or any activity other than the performance of the appraisal

- any management fees charged by an AMC or other third party must be for actual services related to ordering, processing or reviewing of appraisals performed for FHA financing, and

- AMC and other third party fees must not exceed what is customary and reasonable for such services provided in the market area of the property being appraised.

d. Verification of Compliance With Property Requirements

As the on-site representative for the lender, the appraiser provides preliminary verification that a property meets the General Acceptability Standards, which include the Minimum Property Requirements (MPR) or Minimum Property Standards (MPS).

e. Lender Responsibility for Determination of Property Eligibility and Accuracy of Appraised Value

Lenders are responsible for properly reviewing appraisals and determining if the appraised value used to determine the mortgage amount is accurate and adequately supports the value conclusion.

f. Variations in the Property Appraisal and Underwriting Process

The property appraisal and underwriting process varies by stage of construction, and type of processing.

g. Property Eligibility for FHA Insurance

Only one to four unit properties, including a one family unit in a condominium project, are eligible for mortgage insurance, except for mortgage insured under Section 220 of the National Housing Act. The mortgage must be on real estate held:
- in fee simple
- on leasehold under a lease for not less than 99 years which is renewable, or
- under a lease having a period of not less than 10 years to run beyond the maturity date of the mortgage.

For properties processed under the HECM program, the mortgage must be on real estate held
- in fee simple
- on leasehold under a lease for not less than 99 years which is renewable, or
- under a lease having a remaining period of not less than 50 years beyond the date of the 100th birthday of the youngest mortgagor.

h. Property Eligibility Under Section 223(e)

A mortgage may be insured pursuant to Section 223(e) for the repair, rehabilitation, construction, or purchase of properties in older, declining urban areas. Eligibility under Section 223(e) is determined by the appropriate HOC.

If the case is being processed under the Direct Endorsement (DE) Lender Program, the lender must submit the case binder to the appropriate HOC for prior approval processing and Section 223(e) consideration. The case binder must be submitted after the appraiser and the lender's underwriter have determined that:

> • the property does not meet the location eligibility requirements of Section 203(b), but
> • the property is located in an older, declining urban area that may qualify for Section 223(e).

i. Compliance Inspection Requirements

Compliance inspections completed by FHA Roster Inspectors or local authority with jurisdiction may be required for:

> • proposed construction or properties under construction
> • properties undergoing substantial rehabilitation, and
> • existing properties requiring repairs to major systems (for example, structural, heating, and so on).

The number and timing of inspections for new construction depends upon the:

> • stage of construction (proposed construction, under construction, or new construction less than one year old)
> • coverage by an acceptable 10 year warranty plan
> • issuance of a building permit and Certificate of Occupancy (CO) by the local jurisdiction
> • acceptability of inspections by the local community, and
> • the type of construction (stick built, manufactured home, or condominium conversions). Modular homes are treated the same as stick built.

A clear final inspection or, in certain cases, a Certificate of Occupancy, will be required before FHA will insure the mortgage. Part B, Certificate of Completion, of Fannie Mae Form 1004D/Freddie Mac Form 442 provides for compliance repair and completion inspections for existing and new construction dwellings.

j. Appraisal Assignment to Ensure Appraiser Competency

An appraiser who is primarily experienced in appraising detached, single family dwellings in one market may lack the knowledge, experience and/or resources for obtaining market data that will enable the appraiser to perform quality appraisals on condominiums or manufactured homes in the same market, or on detached, single family homes in another market a short distance away.

The valuation principles for appraising all residential properties are essentially the same, no matter the market in which the property is located. However not all appraisers are knowledgeable and experienced, or have access to sources of data for all markets.

The lender must select an appropriate appraiser for every assignment, one who has knowledge of the market area, or geographic competency.

A lender must not assume, simply because an appraiser is state-certified, that the appraiser is qualified and knowledgeable in a specific market area or property type. It is incumbent upon the lender to determine whether an appraiser's qualifications, as evidenced by educational training and actual field experience, are sufficient to enable the appraiser to competently perform appraisals before assigning an appraisal to him/her.

k. Preventing Improper Influences on Appraisers

In order to help FHA Roster appraisers avoid conflicts of interest or appearance of conflicts of interest, no member of a lender's loan production staff or any person who is compensated on a commission basis tied to the successful completion of a loan, or reports, ultimately, to any officer of the lender not independent of the loan production staff and process, shall have substantive communications with an appraiser relating to or having an impact on valuation, including ordering or managing an appraisal assignment.

l. Prohibition of Mortgage Brokers and Commission based Lender staff from the Appraisal Process

FHA prohibited lenders from accepting appraisal reports completed by an appraiser selected, retained or compensated, in any manner by real estate agents. To ensure appraiser independence, FHA-approved lenders are now prohibited from accepting appraisals prepared by FHA Roster appraisers who are selected, retained or compensated in any manner by a mortgage broker or any member of a lender's staff who is compensated on a commission basis tied to the successful completion of a loan.

m. Appraiser Independence Safeguards

Lenders, and third parties working on behalf of lenders, are prohibited from:

- withholding or threatening to withhold timely payment or partial payment for an appraisal report

- withholding or threatening to withhold future business from an appraiser

- demoting or terminating, or threatening to demote or terminate, an appraiser

- expressly or impliedly promising future business, promotions or increased compensation for an appraiser

- conditioning the ordering of an appraisal report or the payment of an appraisal fee, salary or bonus on the opinion, conclusion or valuation to be reached, or on a preliminary value estimate requested from an appraiser

- requesting that an appraiser provide an estimated, predetermined or desired valuation in an appraisal report prior to the completion of that report

• requesting that an appraiser provide estimated values or comparable sales at any time prior to the appraiser's completion of an appraisal report.

• providing to the appraiser an anticipated, estimated, encouraged or desired value for a subject property or a proposed or target amount to be loaned to the borrower, except that a copy of the sales contract for purchase must be provided

• providing stock or other financial or non-financial benefits to:
  ■ the appraiser
  ■ the appraisal company
  ■ the appraisal management company, or
  ■ any entity or person related to the appraiser, appraisal company or management company

• allowing the removal of an appraiser from a list of qualified appraisers, or the addition of an appraiser to an exclusionary list of qualified appraisers, used by any entity without prompt written notice to such appraiser, which notice shall include written evidence of the appraiser's
  ■ illegal conduct
  ■ violation of the Uniform Standards of Professional Appraisal Practice standards
  ■ violation of state licensing standards, or
  ■ improper or unprofessional behavior or other substantive reason for removal

• ordering, obtaining, using, or paying for a second or subsequent appraisal or automated valuation model (AVM) in connection with a mortgage financing transaction unless
  ■ there is a reasonable basis to believe that the initial appraisal was flawed or tainted and such appraisal is clearly and appropriately noted in the loan file
  ■ such appraisal or automated valuation model is done pursuant to written, pre-established bona fide pre- or post-funding appraisal review or quality control process or underwriting guidelines, and
  ■ the lender adheres to a policy of selecting the most reliable appraisal, rather than the appraisal that states the highest value, or

• any other act or practice that impairs or attempts to impair an appraiser's independence, objectivity or impartiality, or violates law or regulation, including, but not limited to the Truth in Lending Act (TILA) and Regulation Z and USPAP.

Note: If absolute lines of independence cannot be achieved as a result of the lender's small size and limited staff, the lender must be able to clearly demonstrate that it has prudent safeguards in place to isolate its collateral evaluation process from influence or interference by its loan production process.

n. Appraiser Selection in the FHA Connection

Lenders are also responsible for assuring that the appraiser who actually conducted the appraisal is correctly identified in FHA Connection. Lenders who fail to assure that the FHA Connection reflects the correct name will be subject to administrative sanctions.

o. DE Underwriter Responsibility for Quality of Appraisal Report

The DE Underwriter who is responsible for the quality of the appraisal report is allowed to communicate with the appraiser, to request clarifications and discuss components of the appraisal that influence its quality.

The underwriter bears the primary responsibility for determining the eligibility of a property for FHA insurance.

II. General Acceptability Standards and Property Eligibility

a. Basis for Determination of MPS and MPR

The application of MPS for new construction is determined by:
- construction status (proposed construction, under construction, or existing construction less than one-year old), and
- construction type (on-site construction or manufactured housing).

A property is considered "new construction" if it was completed less than one year from the date of the Certificate of Occupancy (CO) or its equivalent.

The application of MPR for an "existing" property is determined by the date of the CO or its equivalent. To be considered "existing" property, it must be over one year from the date of the CO.

b. Property Standards for Houses and MPR for Site Built and Manufactured Housing

The table below contains the general minimum property standards in order for houses and manufactured homes to be eligible for FHA insurance.

Dwelling Type	Property Standards
Housing	**Eligible housing includes** • detached or semi-detached dwellings • row houses • multiplex dwellings, and • individual condominium units. **Important:** If not detached • the dwelling must be separated from an adjoining dwelling by a party or lot line wall extending the full height of the building, and • each living unit must be individually accessible for use and maintenance without trespass on adjoining properties.

Manufactured Homes	A manufactured home is a structure that is

	• transportable in one or more sections
	• designed and constructed to Federal Manufactured Construction and Safety Standards, and
	• so labeled regarding conformance with the Federal Manufactured Home Construction and Safety Standards (MHCSS).
	
	To be eligible for FHA mortgage insurance, the manufactured home must:
	
	• have at least 400 square feet as the minimum floor area
	• be constructed after June 15, 1976, in conformance with the MHCSS, as evidenced by an affixed certification label
	• be classified as real estate (but need not be treated as real estate for purposes of state taxation)
	• be designed to be used as a dwelling with a permanent foundation built to FHA requirements
	• be built and must still be remaining on a permanent chassis
	• have a mortgage that
	  ■ covers both the unit and its site, and
	  ■ has a term of not more than 30 years from the date of amortization, and
	• have a finished grade elevation beneath the home (including the basement) at or above the 100 year flood elevation.

c. Site Condition Standards

The site conditions of a property must be free of health and safety hazards.

d. Lead- Based Paint Standards

If the property was built before 1978:
> • the seller must disclose known information on lead-based paint and lead-based paint hazards before selling the house
> • the sales contracts must include a disclosure form about lead-based paint, and
> • the buyers have up to 10 days from the date of the signing of the sales contract to check for lead.

FHA may insure a mortgage on a house, even with lead-based paint, if defective paint surfaces are treated. However, FHA will not pay the cost to have the lead-based paint removed, treated, or repaired.

e. Services and Facilities Standards

Utilities and other facilities should be independent for each unit and must include:
> • a continuing supply of safe, potable water
> • sanitary facilities and a safe method of sewage disposal
> • heating adequate for health and comfort
> • domestic hot water, and
> • electricity for lighting and equipment.

f. Access Standards

There must be vehicular access to the property by means of an abutting public or private street. If private, there must be a permanent recorded easement and provisions for permanent maintenance. Each property must have access to its rear yard.

g. Restrictions on Non Residential Use

Non residential use must be subordinate to the property's residential use and character, and it may not exceed 25 percent of the total floor area.

The following non residential properties are ineligible for mortgage insurance:

- commercial enterprises
- hotels/motels
- private clubs
- fraternity/sorority houses

- boarding houses
- tourist houses
- bed and breakfast establishments

Exception: Exceptions to this restriction are made for Section 203(k) properties.

h. Rejection of "Existing" or Newly Constructed Property

When examination of "existing" or newly constructed property reveals noncompliance with the General Acceptability Standards, an appropriate specific condition (repair) to correct the deficiency is required, if correction is feasible.

If correction is not feasible, and only major repairs or alterations can affect compliance, the lender must reject the property.

Note: The appraiser must note those repairs necessary to make the property comply with FHA's General Acceptability Standards, together with the estimated cost to cure. The lender will determine which repairs for existing properties must be made for the property to be eligible for FHA-insured financing.

III. Requirements for Properties in Special Flood Hazard Areas (SFHA)

a. Responsibility for Determining Property Eligibility in SFHA

The lender is responsible for determining the eligibility of properties in special flood hazard areas (SFHA) as designated by the Federal Emergency Management Agency (FEMA). The FHA appraiser is required to review the FEMA Flood Insurance Rate Map, note the FEMA zone designation on the Uniform Residential Appraisal Report (URAR), and, if the property is located in a SFHA, attach a copy of the flood map panel. Lenders are strongly encouraged, however, to obtain a flood zone certification independent of any assessment made by the appraiser, to avoid culpability for regulatory violations or civil claims for damages that may arise from improper determinations.

Lenders must inform borrowers of the requirement to obtain adequate flood insurance as a condition of closing for properties where any portion of the dwelling and related structures and equipment are located in a SFHA. They must require the escrow of flood insurance premiums if escrow is required for other items such as hazard insurance and taxes.

b. Properties in SHFA Ineligible for FHA Insurance

A property is not eligible for FHA insurance if a residential building and related improvements to the property are located within a SFHA (Zone A, a "Special Flood Zone Area", or Zone V, a "Coastal Area"), and insurance under the National Flood Insurance Program (NFIP) is not available in the community.

c. Eligibility of Proposed and New Construction in SFHAs

If any portion of the property improvements (the dwelling and related structures/equipment essential to the value of the property and subject to flood damage) is located within a SFHA, the property is not eligible for FHA mortgage insurance unless:

- a final Letter of Map Amendment (LOMA) or final Letter of Map Revision (LOMR) that removes the property from the SFHA is obtained from FEMA, or

- if the property is not removed from the SFHA by a LOMA or LOMR, the lender obtains a FEMA National Flood Insurance Program Elevation Certificate (FEMA form 81-31), prepared by a licensed engineer or surveyor, documenting that the lowest floor (including the basement) of the residential building, and all related improvements/equipment essential to the value of the property, is built at or above the 100-year flood elevation in compliance with the NFIP criteria.

If a LOMA or LOMR is obtained that removes the property from the SFHA, neither flood insurance nor a flood elevation certificate is required.

Insurance under the NFIP is required when a flood elevation certificate documents that the property remains located within a SFHA.

Note: The LOMA, LOMR or flood elevation certificate must be submitted with the case for endorsement.

d. Lender Discretion on Requiring a Flood Elevation Certificate and/or Flood Insurance

If a lender is uncertain about whether a property is located within a SFHA, it may require a flood elevation certificate. In addition, the lender has discretion to require national flood insurance even if:
- the residential building and related improvements to the property are not located within the SFHA, but the lender has reason to believe that the building and related improvements to the property may be vulnerable to damage from flooding.

e. Flood Insurance Requirements for Existing Construction

Insurance under the NFIP must be obtained as a condition of closing and maintained for the life of the loan for an existing property when any portion of the residential improvements is determined to be located in a SFHA. If the improvements are subsequently removed from a SFHA by a LOMA or LOMR, flood insurance will no longer be required.

f. Flood Insurance for Condominiums

The Homeowners' Association (HOA), not the individual condominium owner, is responsible for maintaining flood insurance on buildings located within a SFHA.

The lender is responsible for ensuring that the HOA obtains and maintains adequate flood insurance if the FHA appraiser reports that buildings in a condominium project are located within a SFHA. The flood insurance coverage must protect the interest of borrowers who hold title to individual units as well as the common areas of the condominium project.

A LOMA, LOMR or elevation certificate is acceptable evidence if any part of the property improvements is located within the SFHA.

g. Flood Insurance for Manufactured Homes

If any portion of property improvements for both new and existing manufactured home properties are located within a SFHA (Zones A or V), the property is not eligible for FHA mortgage insurance without:

- a FEMA-issued LOMA or LOMR, or

- an elevation certificate, prepared by a licensed engineer or surveyor on the finished construction, indicating that the finish grade beneath the dwelling or manufactured home is at or above the 100-year return frequency flood elevation.

Note: When utilizing an elevation certificate, the property remains in a SFHA and flood insurance is required. Neither an elevation certificate nor flood insurance is required with LOMA or LOMR that removes the property from the SFHA.

Important: For manufactured homes with basements, the grade beneath the basement must be at or above the 100-year flood elevation.

h. Required Insurance Amount

National flood insurance is required for the term of the loan and must be maintained in an amount equal to the least of the following:

- the development cost of the property, less estimated land cost
- the maximum amount of the NFIP insurance available with respect to the property improvements, or
- the outstanding principal balance of the loan(s).

IV. Appraisal Requirements

a. FHA Policy on Appraisals

Except for certain streamline refinance transactions, FHA requires an appraisal of all properties to establish an estimated value for mortgage insurance purposes.

All individual properties, whether proposed construction, under construction, or existing construction, must meet MPS or MPR.

b. Appraisal Reporting Standards

An appraisal performed for FHA purposes requires that the appraiser:

- address all sections of the appraisal form

- complete the form in a manner that clearly reflects the thoroughness of the investigation and analysis of the appraisal findings, and

- ensure that the conclusions about the observed conditions of the property provide rationale for the opinion of market value.

The completed appraisal form utilized, together with the required exhibits, constitutes the reporting instrument to HUD for FHA-insured mortgages.

c. Appraisal Reporting Forms

The appraisal reporting form used depends on the type of property that is being appraised.

The table below lists the appraisal forms used by the appraiser, depending upon the type of property being appraised.

Important: Regardless of which form in the table below is used, the Fannie Mae Form 1004MC, Market Conditions Addendum, must be completed along with the appropriate appraisal form.

Appraisal Form	Form Usage
Uniform Residential Appraisal Report (URAR) - Fannie Mae Form 1004	Required to report an appraisal of • a one unit property, or • a one unit property with an accessory unit.
Manufactured Home Appraisal Report - Fannie Mae Form 1004C	Required to report an appraisal of a one-unit manufactured home.
Individual Condominium Unit Appraisal Report - Fannie Mae Form 1073	Required to report an appraisal of • a unit in a condominium project, or • a condominium unit in a planned unit development (PUD).

Small Residential Income Property Appraisal Report - Fannie Mae Form 1025	Required to report an appraisal of a two to four unit property.
Manufactured Home Appraisal Report - Fannie Mae Form 1004	Required to report an appraisal of a condominium manufactured home.
Individual Condominium Unit Appraisal Report - Fannie Mae Form 1073	Required as an addendum to the appraisal report if the property is located in a manufactured housing condominium project (MHCP).

Appraisal Update and/or Completion Report - Fannie Mae Form 1004D	This is a dual-purpose form.
	
	• **Part A,** Summary Appraisal Update Report
	  ■ provides for updates of existing appraisals when the appraiser concurs with the original appraisal report, and
	    ■ updates the appraisal by incorporating the original appraisal report.
	
	• **Part B,** Completion Report, provides for compliance repair and completion inspections for existing and new construction dwellings.

d. Term of an Appraisal

The validity period for all appraisals on existing, proposed and under construction properties is 120 days.

If the appropriate HOC determines that soft market conditions exist in certain areas or markets, it may shorten the term of appraisals for substantial rehabilitation upon advance notice to lenders.

The term of the appraisal begins on the day the home is inspected by the FHA-approved appraiser and this date appears on the URAR.

e. FHA Policy on Appraisal Reuse

Appraisals cannot be reused after the mortgage for which the appraisal was ordered has closed.

A new appraisal is required for each refinance transaction requiring an appraisal.

Example: An appraisal used for the purchase of a property cannot be used again for a subsequent refinance, even if six months has not passed.

f. FHA Policy on Appraisal Extensions

If a borrower signs a valid sales contract or is approved for a loan prior to the expiration date of the appraisal, the term of the appraisal may be extended, at the option of the lender, for 30 days to allow for the approval of the borrower and closing of the loan.

Approval of the borrower occurs when the lender's DE underwriter signs the HUD-92900-LT, FHA Loan Underwriting and Transmittal Summary.

g. FHA Policy on Appraisal and Inspection Fees

The lender is responsible for collecting and promptly paying appraisers and inspectors.

h. Lender Responsibility for Providing Appraised Value Documentation to the Borrower

In accordance with the provisions of the National Housing Act, the lender must provide to the borrower a Statement of Appraised Value. The lender accomplishes this by giving the borrower a copy of HUD-92800.5B, Conditional Commitment - DE Statement of Appraised Value, or a copy of the completed appraisal report, at or before loan closing.

i. Appraisal Transfer and Change of Client Name when the Borrower Switches Lenders

In cases where a borrower has switched lenders, the first lender must, at the borrower's request, transfer the case to the second lender. FHA does not require that the client name on the appraisal be changed when it is transferred to another lender.

In accordance with the Uniform Standards of Professional Appraisal Practice (USPAP), the second lender is not permitted to request that the appraiser change the name of the client within the appraisal report unless it is a new appraisal assignment. To effect a client name change, the second lender and the original appraiser may engage in a new appraisal assignment wherein the scope of work is limited to the client name change. A new client name should include the name of the client (lender) and HUD.

j. Ordering a Second Appraisal when the Borrower Switches Lenders

FHA prohibits "appraiser shopping", where lenders order additional appraisals in an effort to assure the highest possible value for the property, and/or the least amount of deficiencies or repairs are noted and required by the appraiser.

However, in the case where a borrower switches from one FHA lender (first lender) to a second lender, and an appraisal was ordered by and completed for the first lender, a second appraisal may be ordered by the second lender if the:

> • first appraisal contains material deficiencies, as determined by the Direct Endorsement underwriter for the second lender
>
> • appraiser performing the first appraisal is on the second lender's exclusionary list of appraisers, or
>
> • failure of the first lender to provide a copy of the appraisal to the second lender in a timely manner would cause a delay in closing, posing potential harm to the borrower, which includes events outside the borrower's control such as:

> > ■ loss of interest rate lock   ■ purchase contract deadline
> > ■ foreclosure proceedings   ■ late fees

For the first two scenarios above, the lender must ensure that copies of both appraisals are retained in the case binder. For the third scenario, the appraisal from the first lender must be added to the case binder when it is received.

Important: In all cases, the lender must document why a second appraisal was ordered and retain the explanation in the case binder.

k. When the Appraisal and/or Completion Report Form Is Used

The FHA appraiser should only use Fannie Mae Form 1004D/Freddie Mac Form 442, Appraisal Update and/or Completion Report under the conditions described in the table below.

When the lender...	Then the appraiser...
• needs to extend the validity period of an existing appraisal that is due to expire, and • does not want to order a new appraisal	should use Part A/Appraisal Update.
needs to extend the validity period of an existing appraisal for new construction that is incomplete	should use Part A/Appraisal Update.
needs to report the • completion of a repair, and/or • satisfaction of requirements and conditions noted on the original appraisal report referenced in the header of the Summary Appraisal Update and/or Completion Report	should use Part B/Completion Report.

l. When the Appraisal and/or Completion Report Form Is Not Used

The FHA appraiser may not use Fannie Mae Form 1004D/Freddie Mac Form 442, Appraisal Update and/or Completion Report under the conditions described in the table below.

If ...	Then the appraiser...
• the property has declined in value • the building improvements that contribute value to the property cannot be observed from the street or a public way, or • the exterior inspection of the property reveals deficiencies or other significant changes that did not exist as of the effective date of the appraisal report being updated	may not use Part A/Appraisal Update.
• the property is new construction and manufactured housing, and • a form HUD-92051, Compliance Inspection Report, is required	may not use Part B/Completion Report.

m. Who May Use the Appraisal Update and/or Completion Report Form

The FHA appraiser who performed the original appraisal, if currently in good standing on the FHA Appraiser Roster, may use Part A, Summary Appraisal Update Report, or Part B, Completion Report.

Any other FHA appraiser, currently in good standing on the FHA Appraiser Roster, may only use Part B, Completion Report.

V. Appraisal Repair Requirements

a. FHA Policy on Appraisal Repair Requirements

In the performance of an FHA appraisal, the appraiser must denote any deficiency in the appropriate section(s) of the appraisal report (site issues in the site section, improvement issues in the improvements section, and so on), and note those repairs necessary to make the property comply with FHA's MPR, or MPS, together with the estimated cost to cure.

The lender determines which repairs for existing properties must be made for the property to be eligible for FHA-insured financing.

b. Types of Repairs

The types of repairs that may need to be made to a property include cosmetic repairs, and required repairs. The table below describes cosmetic and required repairs.

Type of Repair	Description
Cosmetic repairs	These repairs are not required, however, they must be considered in the overall condition rating and valuation of the property. Such repairs would include surface treatments, beautification or adornment not required for the preservation of the property. Generally, worn floor finishes or carpets, holes in window screens, or a small crack in a windowpane are examples of deferred maintenance that do not rise to the level of a required repair, but must be reported by the appraiser.
Required repairs	The physical condition of existing building improvements must be examined at the time of the appraisal to determine whether repairs, alterations or inspection are necessary or essential to eliminating conditions that threaten the continued physical security of the property. Required repairs must be limited to those required to • protect the health and safety of the occupants (Safety) • protect the security of the property (Security), and • correct physical deficiencies or conditions affecting structural integrity (Soundness).

c. Properties With Defective Conditions

A property with defective conditions is unacceptable for FHA insurance until the conditions have been remedied and the probability of further damage has been eliminated. Defective conditions include:
- defective construction, and
- other readily observable conditions that impair the safety, security, or structural soundness of the dwelling.

d. Additional Required Inspections by Qualified Entities

Typical conditions that would require further inspection or testing by qualified individuals or entities include:
- infestation - evidence of termites
- inoperative or inadequate plumbing, heating, or electrical systems
- structural failure in framing members
- leaking or worn-out roofs
- cracked masonry or foundation damage, and
- drainage problems.

VI. Satisfying Repair Requirements

a. FHA Policy on Satisfying Repair Requirements

Repair requirements outstanding on the appraisal report must be satisfied before the mortgage is submitted for endorsement. Satisfaction of repair requirements can be submitted by providing:
- a Compliance Inspection Report (HUD-92051)
- Part B of Fannie Mae Form 1004D/Freddie Mac Form 442, Appraisal Update and/or Completion Report
- the Mortgagee's Assurance of Completion (HUD-92300) of escrowed repairs, or
- a certification from a "qualified" professional on their company form or letterhead.

Note: A "qualified" professional may be a professionally licensed engineer, home inspector, or trades person.

b. Compliance Inspection Report

Form HUD-92051, Compliance Inspection Report, or Part B of Fannie Mae Form 1004D/Freddie Mac Form 442, Appraisal Update and/or Completion Report, are used to certify that repairs have been completed satisfactorily.

Part B of Fannie Mae Form 1004D/Freddie Mac Form 442, Appraisal Update and/or Completion Report provides for compliance repair and compliance inspections for existing and new construction dwellings. **Important:** Part B of Fannie Mae Form 1004D/Freddie Mac Form 442 may not be used in lieu of Form HUD-92051, Compliance Inspection Report, for new construction and manufactured housing.

These forms must be prepared, as appropriate, by: an appraiser or an FHA fee inspector, for inspections that require architectural expertise (such as structural or basic system repair). **Note:** An FHA-approved inspector list is available via the FHA Connection.

c. Lender Certification

A lender certification HUD-92300, Mortgagee's Assurance of Completion is acceptable in those instances in which the required repair items are minor and uncomplicated.

Note: If the borrower could complete the work on his/her own as normal maintenance, FHA considers the work to be "minor".

d. Escrow of Funds for Completion of Construction

If adverse weather conditions prevent completion of the repairs, it is not always necessary to complete all new construction items (for example, landscaping) or required repairs (such as exterior painting) before submitting the mortgage for insurance endorsement. In certain situations, funds may be escrowed, and FHA will accept a HUD-92300, Mortgagee's Assurance of Completion at the time of endorsement.

The escrow of funds may only be used when:
- the dwelling is habitable, safe and essentially complete
- the deferred work cannot be acceptably completed prior to loan closing, but will be completed within six months
- all other conditions of the appraisal have been satisfied by compliance inspections or by an acceptable Mortgagee's Assurance of Completion, and
- the lender has not been denied the privilege of using a Mortgagee's Assurance of Completion due to poor follow up or non satisfaction of outstanding escrows.

e. Lender Obligation to Complete Improvements Regardless of Escrow Reserves

The lender assumes the obligation to satisfactorily complete improvements, regardless of the adequacy of the funds reserved by escrow or letter of credit.

An appraiser or an inspector on FHA's Appraiser Roster or FHA's Panel of Inspectors must confirm that the work was satisfactorily completed.

VII. Prohibition on Property Flipping

a. Definition: Property Flipping

The term property flipping refers to a practice whereby recently acquired property is resold for a considerable profit with an artificially inflated value, often abetted by a lender's collusion with an appraiser.

b. Inapplicability of Property Flipping Restrictions to New Construction

The restrictions listed in this topic do not apply to a builder selling a newly built home or building a home for a borrower wishing to use FHA-insured financing.

c. Seller Must Be the Owner of Record

To be eligible for a mortgage insured by FHA:
- a property must be purchased from the owner of record
- the transaction may not involve any sale or assignment of the sales contract, and
- the lender must obtain, and submit in the case binder to HUD, documentation verifying that the seller is the owner or record.

Such documentation may include, but is not limited to:
- a property sales history report
- a copy of the recorded deed from the seller, or
- other documentation, such as a copy of a property tax bill, title commitment, or binder, demonstrating the seller's ownership of the property and the date it was acquired.

Note: This requirement applies to all FHA purchase money mortgages, regardless of the time between re-sales.

d. Appraiser Responsibility for Analyzing Prior Sales of a Property

To be in compliance with updated Standard Rule 1-5 of the Uniform Standards of Professional Appraisal Practice (USPAP), appraisers are required to analyze any prior sales of a subject property in the previous three years for one to four family residential properties.

Mortgage lenders may rely on the information provided by the appraiser in the Uniform Residential Appraisal Report (URAR) describing the Date, Price and Data for Prior Sales for the subject property within the last three years.

e. Restriction on Re- Sales Occurring 90 Days or Less After Acquisition

If a property is re-sold 90 days or fewer following the date of acquisition by the seller, the property is not eligible for a mortgage insured by FHA.

FHA defines the:

- seller's date of acquisition as the date of settlement on the seller's purchase of that property, and

- re-sale date as the date of execution of the sales contract by a buyer intending to finance the property with an FHA-insured loan.

f. Second Appraisal Required on Properties Sold Between 91 and 180 Days After Acquisition

A lender must obtain a second appraisal by another appraiser if:

- the re-sale date of a property is between 91 and 180 days following the acquisition of the property by the seller, and

- the resale price is 100 percent or more over the price paid by the seller when the property was acquired.

FHA reserves the right to revise the resale percentage level at which this second appraisal is required by publishing a notice in the Federal Register.

Example: If a property is re-sold for $80,000 within six months of the seller's acquisition of that property for $40,000, the lender must obtain a second independent appraisal supporting the $80,000 sales price. Even if the lender provides documentation showing the cost and extent of rehabilitation that went into the property resulting in the increased value, the second appraisal is still required.

Note: The cost of the second appraisal may not be charged to the borrower.

g. Resales Occurring Between 91 Days and 12 Months Following Acquisition

FHA reserves the right to require additional documentation from a lender to support the resale value of a property if:
- the resale date is more than 90 days after the date of acquisition by the seller, but before the end of the twelfth month following the date of acquisition, and

- the resale price is 5 percent or greater than the lowest sale price of the property during the preceding 12 months.

At FHA's discretion, such documentation may include, but not be limited to, an appraisal from another appraiser.

h. Exceptions to the 90 Day Restriction

The only exceptions to the 90 day resale restriction are for:

- properties acquired by an employer or relocation agency in connection with the relocation of an employee

- re-sales by HUD under its Real Estate Owned (REO) program

- sales by other United States Government agencies of single family properties pursuant to programs operated by these agencies

- sales of properties by nonprofits approved to purchase HUD owned single family properties at a discount with resale restrictions

- sales of properties that are acquired by the seller by inheritance

- sales of properties by state and federally-chartered financial institutions and government sponsored enterprises

- sales of properties by local and state government agencies, and

- sales of properties within Presidentially Declared Disaster Areas.

Any subsequent re-sales of the properties described above must meet the 90 day threshold in order for the mortgage to be eligible as security for FHA insurance.

Note: HOCs do not have the authority to waive the 90-day resale restriction because it is a regulatory requirement and not an administrative policy.

VIII. Seller Concessions and Verification of Sales

a. FHA Policy on Appraisal Requirements for Sales Concessions

Sales concessions influence the price paid for real estate. For this reason, FHA requires that appraisers identify and report sales concessions and properly address and/or adjust the comparable sale transactions to account for sales concessions in the appraisal of all properties to be security for an FHA-insured loan.

b. Types of Sales Concessions

Sales concessions may be in the form of any of the following concessions given by the seller or any other party involved in a mortgage transaction:

- loan discount points
- interest rate buy downs
- payment of condominium fees
- down payment assistance
- personal property

- loan origination fees
- closing cost assistance
- builder incentives
- monetary gifts, or

c. Lender Requirements Regarding Sales Concessions

FHA requires that lenders comply with the requirements listed below with respect to sales concessions:

- on any real estate purchase transaction, the lender must provide the appraiser with a complete copy of the ratified sales contract, including all addenda, for the subject property that is to be appraised

• lenders must provide appraisers with all financing data and sales concessions for the subject property granted by anyone associated with the transaction (Note: Sales concession information must include gifts and/or down payment assistance, which may or may not be included in the contract of sale.), and

• if a lender requests a reconsideration of value, the lender must provide the appraiser with any amendments to the contract that occurred after the effective date of the appraisal.

Note: Contributions from sellers or other interested third parties to the transaction that exceed 6 percent of the sales price or other financing concessions must be treated as inducements to purchase, thereby reducing the amount of the mortgage.

IX. Reporting Requirements for Appraisals in Declining Markets

a. Description of "Declining Market" for Purposes of Properties That Are Collateral for an FHA-Insured Mortgage

While there is no standard industry definition, for purposes of performing appraisals on properties that are to be collateral for FHA-insured mortgages, a "declining market" is considered to be any neighborhood, market area, or region that demonstrates a decline in prices or deterioration in other market conditions as evidenced by an oversupply of existing inventory or extended marketing times

Note: A declining trend in the market must be identified by the conclusions of the Fannie Mae 1004MC, Market Conditions Addendum. The appraiser must provide a summary comment and provide support for all conclusions relating to the trend of the current market.

b. Policy Requiring Use of Comparables for Appraisal Reporting in Declining Markets

In order to show recent market activity, appraisals of properties located in declining markets must include at least two comparable sales that:

• closed within 90 days prior to the effective date of the appraisal, and
• are as similar as possible to the subject property.

Note: In cases where compliance with this requirement is difficult or not possible due to the lack of market data, a detailed explanation is required.

c. Specific Requirements for Reporting Comparable Listings/ Pending Sales for Appraisals in Declining Markets

In order to ensure that FHA receives an accurate and thorough appraisal analysis, the inclusion of comparable listings and/or pending sales is required in appraisals of properties that are located in declining markets. Specifically, the appraiser must:

• include a minimum of two active listings or pending sales on the appraisal grid of the applicable appraisal reporting form in comparable 4-6 position or higher (in addition to the three settled sales)

• ensure that active listings and pending sales are market tested and have reasonable market exposure to avoid the use of over priced properties as comparables. (Note: Reasonable market exposure is reflected by typical marketing times for the neighborhood. The comparable listings should be truly comparable and the appraiser should bracket the listings using both dwelling size and sales price whenever possible.)

• adjust active listings to reflect list to sale price ratios for the market

• adjust pending sales to reflect the contract purchase price whenever possible or adjust pending sales to reflect list to sale price ratios

• include the original list price, any revised list prices, and total days on the market (DOM) (Note: Provide an explanation for DOM that do not approximate time frames reported in the Neighborhood section of the appraisal reporting form or that do not coincide with the DOM noted in the Market Conditions Addendum.)

• reconcile the adjusted values of active listings or pending sales with the adjusted values of the settled sales provided (Note: If the adjusted values of the settled comparables are higher than the adjusted values of the active listings or pending sales, the appraiser must determine if a market condition adjustment is appropriate. The final value conclusion should not be based solely on the comparable listing or pending sales data.), and

• include an absorption rate analysis, which is critical to developing and supporting market trend conclusions, as mandated by the Market Conditions Addendum. (Example: Assuming 36 sales during a six-month period, the absorption rate is 6 sales per month (36/6).

d. Specific Requirements for Market Trend Data Sources

Data regarding market trends is available from a number of local and nationwide sources. Appraisers must be diligent in using only impartial sources of data. The appraiser must:

- • verify data via local parties to the transaction, such as
  - agents
  - sellers
  - buyers
  - lenders

• use public records or another impartial data source that can be replicated if a sale cannot be verified by a party.

Unacceptable Sources:

Unacceptable data sources include local and national media and other sources considered not readily verifiable. A Multiple Listing Service (MLS) by itself is not considered a verification source.

Note: Appraisal results should be able to be replicated. Known or reported incentives or sales concessions must be noted in the financing section of the grid for any active or pending comparable used.

X. Property Eligibility Requirements Specific to Manufactured Homes

a. Foundation Requirements for Manufactured Homes

All manufactured home permanent foundation systems must follow the FHA guidelines in effect at the time of the certification, which are currently published in the Permanent Foundations Guide for Manufactured Housing (PFGMH).

b. Engineer's Certification on Foundation Compliance for Manufactured Homes

The lender must submit an Engineer's Certification on Foundation Compliance, attesting to compliance with the current PFGMH, which must be:
- completed by a licensed professional engineer or registered architect, who is licensed/registered in the state where the manufactured home is located
- site-specific, and
- included in both the lender's loan file and the insuring binder when submitted to FHA.

Note: The certification must contain the engineer's or registered architect's signature, seal, and/or state license/certification number. In states where seals are issued, the seal must be on the certification.

c. Use of the Engineer's Certification on Foundation Compliance for Manufactured Homes for Future Loans

A copy of the foundation certification, showing that the foundation met the PFGMH guidelines that were in effect at the time of certification, is acceptable for future FHA loans, provided there are no alterations and/or observable damage to the foundation.

A copy of the foundation certification is not required in the loan file or insuring binder for any:

- FHA-to-FHA transaction, provided that no modifications have been made to the foundation or structure from the date of the effective certification, or

- FHA/HUD Real Estate Owned (REO) Division sales.

d. Perimeter Enclosures for Manufactured Homes

For the space beneath a manufactured home to be properly enclosed, the perimeter enclosure must:
- be a continuous wall (whether bearing or non-load bearing)
- be adequately secured to the perimeter of the unit
- separate the crawl space from backfill

- keeps out vermin and water, and
- allow for proper ventilation of the crawl space.

For new construction, the space beneath the home shall be enclosed by a continuous foundation-type construction designed to resist all forces to which it is subjected without transmitting forces to the building superstructure. The enclosure shall be constructed of materials that conform to the PFGMH, and to HUD Minimum Property Standards (MPS), such as concrete, masonry, or treated wood.

For existing construction, there must be adequate backing, such as concrete, masonry, or treated wood, to permanently attach and support or reinforce the skirting, if the perimeter enclosure is non-load bearing skirting comprised of lightweight material.

e. Required Inspections for New Construction Manufactured Homes

For newly-constructed manufactured homes, initial and final inspections must be completed in accordance with Architectural Processing and Inspections for Home Mortgage Insurance; and reported using the Compliance Inspection Report form. The inspections must be performed by:
- FHA Compliance Inspectors
- licensed engineers
- registered architects, or
- other qualified construction industry professionals, as determined by the lender.

The inspector must have a copy of the FHA-required foundation certification, and related plans and specifications at the time of the inspection.

FHA Roster appraisers may use Part B of Fannie Mae Form 1004D/Freddie Mac Form 442, Appraisal Update and/or Completion Report, which provides for compliance repair and completion inspections for existing and new construction dwellings.

Important: The FNMA form Fannie Mae Form 1004D/Freddie Mac Form 442, Appraisal Update and/or Completion Report may not be used in lieu of form HUD-92051, Compliance Inspection Report, for new construction and manufactured housing.

f. Termite Control for Manufactured Homes

The steel chassis under a newly-constructed manufactured home unit is not an effective termite barrier. Any one, or a combination of the following methods is required for maximum protection against termites, including
- chemical soil treatment
- EPA-registered bait treatments
- pressure preservative-treated wood, or
- naturally termite-resistant wood.

Termite protection policies for existing manufactured homes will be handled in the same manner as stick-built homes. State or local requirements are to be followed.

Glossary

203(b): FHA's single family program which provides mortgage insurance to lenders to protect against the borrower defaulting; 203(b) is used to finance the purchase of new or existing one to four family housing; 203(b) insured loans are known for requiring a low down payment, flexible qualifying guidelines, limited fees, and a limit on maximum loan amount.

203(k): this FHA mortgage insurance program enables homebuyers to finance both the purchase of a house and the cost of its rehabilitation through a single mortgage loan.

"A" Loan or "A" Paper: a credit rating where the FICO score is 660 or above. There have been no late mortgage payments within a 12-month period. This is the best credit rating to have when entering into a new loan.

ARM: Adjustable Rate Mortgage; a mortgage loan subject to changes in interest rates; when rates change, ARM monthly payments increase or decrease at intervals determined by the lender; the change in monthly payment amount, however, is usually subject to a cap.

Abstract of Title: documents recording the ownership of property throughout time.

Acceleration: the right of the lender to demand payment on the outstanding balance of a loan.

Acceptance: the written approval of the buyer's offer by the seller.

Additional Principal Payment: money paid to the lender in addition to the established payment amount used directly against the loan principal to shorten the length of the loan.

Adjustable-Rate Mortgage (ARM): a mortgage loan that does not have a fixed interest rate. During the life of the loan the interest rate will change based on the index rate. Also referred to as adjustable mortgage loans (AMLs) or variable-rate mortgages (VRMs).

Adjustment Date: the actual date that the interest rate is changed for an ARM.

Adjustment Index: the published market index used to calculate the interest rate of an ARM at the time of origination or adjustment.

Adjustment Interval: the time between the interest rate change and the monthly payment for an ARM. The interval is usually every one, three or five years depending on the index.

Affidavit: a signed, sworn statement made by the buyer or seller regarding the truth of information provided.

Amenity: a feature of the home or property that serves as a benefit to the buyer but that is not necessary to its use; may be natural (like location, woods, water) or man-made (like a swimming pool or garden).

American Society of Home Inspectors: the American Society of Home Inspectors is a professional association of independent home inspectors.

Amortization: a payment plan that enables you to reduce your debt gradually through monthly payments. The payments may be principal and interest, or interest-only. The monthly amount is based on the schedule for the entire term or length of the loan.

Annual Mortgagor Statement: yearly statement to borrowers detailing the remaining principal and amounts paid for taxes and interest.

Annual Percentage Rate (APR): a measure of the cost of credit, expressed as a yearly rate. It includes interest as well as other charges. Because all lenders, by federal law, follow the same rules to ensure the accuracy of the annual percentage rate, it provides consumers with a good basis for comparing the cost of loans, including mortgage plans. APR is a higher rate than the simple interest of the mortgage.

Application: the first step in the official loan approval process; this form is used to record important information about the potential borrower necessary to the underwriting process.

Application Fee: a fee charged by lenders to process a loan application.

Appraisal: a document from a professional that gives an estimate of a property's fair market value based on the sales of comparable homes in the area and the features of a property; an appraisal is generally required by a lender before loan approval to ensure that the mortgage loan amount is not more than the value of the property.

Appraisal Fee: fee charged by an appraiser to estimate the market value of a property.

Appraised Value: an estimation of the current market value of a property.

Appraiser: a qualified individual who uses his or her experience and knowledge to prepare the appraisal estimate.

Appreciation: an increase in property value.

Arbitration: a legal method of resolving a dispute without going to court.

As-is Condition: the purchase or sale of a property in its existing condition without repairs.

Asking Price: a seller's stated price for a property.

Assessed Value: the value that a public official has placed on any asset (used to determine taxes).

Assessments: the method of placing value on an asset for taxation purposes.

Assessor: a government official who is responsible for determining the value of a property for the purpose of taxation.

Assets: any item with measurable value.

Assumable Mortgage: when a home is sold, the seller may be able to transfer the mortgage to the new buyer. This means the mortgage is assumable. Lenders generally require a credit review of the new borrower and may charge a fee for the assumption. Some mortgages contain a due-on-sale clause, which means that the mortgage may not be transferable to a new buyer. Instead, the lender may make you pay the entire balance that is due when you sell the home.

Assumption Clause: a provision in the terms of a loan that allows the buyer to take legal responsibility for the mortgage from the seller.

Automated Underwriting: loan processing completed through a computer-based system that evaluates past credit history to determine if a loan should be approved. This system removes the possibility of personal bias against the buyer.

Average Price: determining the cost of a home by totaling the cost of all houses sold in one area and dividing by the number of homes sold.

"B" Loan or "B" Paper: FICO scores from 620 - 659.

Factors include two 30 day late mortgage payments and two to three 30 day late installment loan payments in the last 12 months. No delinquencies over 60 days are allowed. Should be two to four years since a bankruptcy. Also referred to as Sub-Prime.

Back End Ratio (debt ratio): a ratio that compares the total of all monthly debt payments (mortgage, real estate taxes and insurance, car loans, and other consumer loans) to gross monthly income.

Back to Back Escrow: arrangements that an owner makes to oversee the sale of one property and the purchase of another at the same time.

Balance Sheet: a financial statement that shows the assets, liabilities and net worth of an individual or company.

Balloon Loan or Mortgage: a mortgage that typically offers low rates for an initial period of time (usually 5, 7, or 10) years; after that time period elapses, the balance is due or is refinanced by the borrower.

Balloon Payment: the final lump sum payment due at the end of a balloon mortgage.

Bankruptcy: a federal law whereby a person's assets are turned over to a trustee and used to pay off outstanding debts; this usually occurs when someone owes more than they have the ability to repay.

Biweekly Payment Mortgage: a mortgage paid twice a month instead of once a month, reducing the amount of interest to be paid on the loan.

Borrower: a person who has been approved to receive a loan and is then obligated to repay it and any additional fees according to the loan terms.

Bridge Loan: a short-term loan paid back relatively fast. Normally used until a long-term loan can be processed.

Broker: a licensed individual or firm that charges a fee to serve as the mediator between the buyer and seller. Mortgage brokers are individuals in the business of arranging funding or negotiating contracts for a client, but who does not loan the money. A real estate broker is someone who helps find a house.

Building Code: based on agreed upon safety standards within a specific area, a building code is a regulation that determines the design, construction, and materials used in building.

Budget: a detailed record of all income earned and spent during a specific period of time.

Buy Down: the seller pays an amount to the lender so the lender provides a lower rate and lower payments many times for an ARM. The seller may increase the sales price to cover the cost of the buy down.

"C" Loan or "C" Paper: FICO scores typically from 580 to 619. Factors include three to four 30 day late mortgage payments and four to six 30 day late installment loan payments or two to four 60 day late payments. Should be one to two years since bankruptcy. Also referred to as Sub-prime.

CAIVRS: CAIVRS is a Federal government database of delinquent Federal debtors that allows federal agencies to reduce the risk to federal loan and loan guarantee programs. CAIVRS alerts participating Federal lending agencies when an applicant for credit benefits, or for a position of trust in support of the administration of a Federal credit program, has a Federal lien, judgment or a Federal loan that is currently in default or foreclosure, or has had a claim paid by a reporting agency.

Callable Debt: a debt security whose issuer has the right to redeem the security at a specified price on or after a specified date, but prior to its stated final maturity.

Cap: a limit, such as one placed on an adjustable rate mortgage, on how much a monthly payment or interest rate can increase or decrease, either at each adjustment period or during the life of the mortgage. Payment caps do not limit the amount of interest the lender is earning, so they may cause negative amortization.

Capacity: The ability to make mortgage payments on time, dependant on assets and the amount of income each month after paying housing costs, debts and other obligations.

Capital Gain: the profit received based on the difference of the original purchase price and the total sale price.

Capital Improvements: property improvements that either will enhance the property value or will increase the useful life of the property.

Capital or Cash Reserves: an individual's savings, investments, or assets.

Cash-Out Refinance: when a borrower refinances a mortgage at a higher principal amount to get additional money. Usually this occurs when the property has appreciated in value. For example, if a home has a current value of $100,000 and an outstanding mortgage of $60,000, the owner could refinance $80,000 and have additional $20,000 in cash.

Cash Reserves: a cash amount sometimes required of the buyer to be held in reserve in addition to the down payment and closing costs; the amount is determined by the lender.

Casualty Protection: property insurance that covers any damage to the home and personal property either inside or outside the home.

Certificate of Title: a document provided by a qualified source, such as a title company, that shows the property legally belongs to the current owner; before the title is transferred at closing, it should be clear and free of all liens or other claims.

Chapter 7 Bankruptcy: a bankruptcy that requires assets be liquidated in exchange for the cancellation of debt.

Chapter 13 Bankruptcy: this type of bankruptcy sets a payment plan between the borrower and the creditor monitored by the court. The homeowner can keep the property, but must make payments according to the court's terms within a 3 to 5 year period.

Charge-Off: the portion of principal and interest due on a loan that is written off when deemed to be uncollectible.

CHUMS: Computerized Homes Underwriting Management System (CHUMS), the system of record for the endorsement process. Large lenders with Loan Origination Systems (LOS) transmit data from their LOS or use third party software to send data to CHUMS via a telecommunications method known as B2G (Business to Government).

Clear Title: a property title that has no defects. Properties with clear titles are marketable for sale.

Closing: the final step in property purchase where the title is transferred from the seller to the buyer. Closing occurs at a meeting between the buyer, seller, settlement agent, and other agents. At the closing the seller receives payment for the property. Also known as settlement.

Closing Costs: fees for final property transfer not included in the price of the property. Typical closing costs include charges for the mortgage loan such as origination fees, discount points, appraisal fee, survey, title insurance, legal fees, real estate professional fees, prepayment of taxes and insurance, and real estate transfer taxes. A common estimate of a Buyer's closing costs is 2 to 4 percent of the purchase price of the home. A common estimate for Seller's closing costs is 3 to 9 percent.

Cloud On The Title: any condition which affects the clear title to real property.

Co-Borrower: an additional person that is responsible for loan repayment and is listed on the title.

Co-Signed Account: an account signed by someone in addition to the primary borrower, making both people responsible for the amount borrowed.

Co-Signer: a person that signs a credit application with another person, agreeing to be equally responsible for the repayment of the loan.

Collateral: security in the form of money or property pledged for the payment of a loan. For example, on a home loan, the home is the collateral and can be taken away from the borrower if mortgage payments are not made.

Collection Account: an unpaid debt referred to a collection agency to collect on the bad debt. This type of account is reported to the credit bureau and will show on the borrower's credit report.

Commission: an amount, usually a percentage of the property sales price that is collected by a real estate professional as a fee for negotiating the transaction. Traditionally the home seller pays the commission. The amount of commission is determined by the real estate professional and the seller and can be as much as 6% of the sales price.

Common Stock: a security that provides voting rights in a corporation and pays a dividend after preferred stock holders have been paid. This is the most common stock held within a company.

Comparative Market Analysis (COMPS): a property evaluation that determines property value by comparing similar properties sold within the last year.

Compensating Factors: factors that show the ability to repay a loan based on less traditional criteria, such as employment, rent, and utility payment history.

Condominium: a form of ownership in which individuals purchase and own a unit of housing in a multi-unit complex. The owner also shares financial responsibility for common areas.

Conforming loan: is a loan that does not exceed Fannie Mae's and Freddie Mac's loan limits. Freddie Mac and Fannie Mae loans are referred to as conforming loans.

Consideration: an item of value given in exchange for a promise or act.

Construction Loan: a short-term, to finance the cost of building a new home. The lender pays the builder based on milestones accomplished during the building process. For example, once a sub-contractor pours the foundation and it is approved by inspectors the lender will pay for their service.

Contingency: a clause in a purchase contract outlining conditions that must be fulfilled before the contract is executed. Both, buyer or seller may include contingencies in a contract, but both parties must accept the contingency.

Conventional Loan: a private sector loan, one that is not guaranteed or insured by the U.S. government.

Conversion Clause: a provision in some ARMs allowing it to change to a fixed-rate loan at some point during the term. Usually conversions are allowed at the end of the first adjustment period. At the time of the conversion, the new fixed rate is generally set at one of the rates then prevailing for fixed rate mortgages. There may be additional cost for this clause.

Convertible ARM: an adjustable-rate mortgage that provides the borrower the ability to convert to a fixed-rate within a specified time.

Cooperative (Co-op): residents purchase stock in a cooperative corporation that owns a structure; each stockholder is then entitled to live in a specific unit of the structure and is responsible for paying a portion of the loan.

Cost of Funds Index (COFI): an index used to determine interest rate changes for some adjustable-rate mortgages.

Counter Offer: a rejection to all or part of a purchase offer that negotiates different terms to reach an acceptable sales contract.

Covenants: legally enforceable terms that govern the use of property. These terms are transferred with the property deed. Discriminatory covenants are illegal and unenforceable. Also known as a condition, restriction, deed restriction or restrictive covenant.

Credit: an agreement that a person will borrow money and repay it to the lender over time.

Credit Bureau: an agency that provides financial information and payment history to lenders about potential borrowers. Also known as a National Credit Repository.

Credit Counseling: education on how to improve bad credit and how to avoid having more debt than can be repaid.

Credit Enhancement: a method used by a lender to reduce default of a loan by requiring collateral, mortgage insurance, or other agreements.

Credit Grantor: the lender that provides a loan or credit.

Credit History: a record of an individual that lists all debts and the payment history for each. The report that is generated from the history is called a credit report. Lenders use this information to gauge a potential borrower's ability to repay a loan.

Credit Loss Ratio: the ratio of credit-related losses to the dollar amount of MBS outstanding and total mortgages owned by the corporation.

Credit Related Expenses: foreclosed property expenses plus the provision for losses.

Credit Related Losses: foreclosed property expenses combined with charge-offs.

Credit Repair Companies: Private, for-profit businesses that claim to offer consumers credit and debt repayment difficulties assistance with their credit problems and a bad credit report.

Credit Report: a report generated by the credit bureau that contains the borrower's credit history for the past seven years. Lenders use this information to determine if a loan will be granted.

Credit Risk: a term used to describe the possibility of default on a loan by a borrower.

Credit Score: a score calculated by using a person's credit report to determine the likelihood of a loan being repaid on time. Scores range from about 360 - 840. A lower score meaning a person is a higher risk, while a higher score means that there is less risk.

Creditor: the lending institution providing a loan or credit.

Creditworthiness: the way a lender measures the ability of a person to qualify and repay a loan.

Debtor: The person or entity that borrows money. The term debtor may be used interchangeably with the term borrower.

Debt-to-Income Ratio: a comparison or ratio of gross income to housing and non-housing expenses; With the FHA, the-monthly mortgage payment should be no more than 29% of monthly gross income (before taxes) and the mortgage payment combined with non-housing debts should not exceed 41% of income.

Debt Security: a security that represents a loan from an investor to an issuer. The issuer in turn agrees to pay interest in addition to the principal amount borrowed.

Deductible: the amount of cash payment that is made by the insured (the homeowner) to cover a portion of a damage or loss. Sometimes also called "out-of-pocket expenses." For example, out of a total damage claim of $1,000, the homeowner might pay a $250 deductible toward the loss, while the insurance company pays $750 toward the loss. Typically, the higher the deductible, the lower the cost of the policy.

Deed: a document that legally transfers ownership of property from one person to another. The deed is recorded on public record with the property description and the owner's signature. Also known as the title.

Deed-in-Lieu: to avoid foreclosure ("in lieu" of foreclosure), a deed is given to the lender to fulfill the obligation to repay the debt; this process does not allow the borrower to remain in the house but helps avoid the costs, time, and effort associated with foreclosure.

Default: the inability to make timely monthly mortgage payments or otherwise comply with mortgage terms. A loan is considered in default when payment has not been paid after 60 to 90 days. Once in default the lender can exercise legal rights defined in the contract to begin foreclosure proceedings.

Delinquency: failure of a borrower to make timely mortgage payments under a loan agreement. Generally after fifteen days a late fee may be assessed.

Deposit (Earnest Money): money put down by a potential buyer to show that they are serious about purchasing the home; it becomes part of the down payment if the offer is accepted, is returned if the offer is rejected, or is forfeited if the buyer pulls out of the deal. During the contingency period the money may be returned to the buyer if the contingencies are not met to the buyer's satisfaction.

Depreciation: a decrease in the value or price of a property due to changes in market conditions, wear and tear on the property, or other factors.

Derivative: a contract between two or more parties where the security is dependent on the price of another investment.

Desktop Underwriter - Desktop Underwriter (DU) is Fannie Mae's automated mortgage loan underwriting system, which was developed to help lenders make informed lending decisions on conventional conforming, FHA and VA loans.

Direct Endorsement (DE) - A certification process for underwriters that allows lenders to underwrite FHA loans in lieu of submitting them to FHA for an underwriting decision.

Disclosures: the release of relevant information about a property that may influence the final sale, especially if it represents defects or problems. "Full disclosure" usually refers to the responsibility of the seller to voluntarily provide all known information about the property. Some disclosures may be required by law, such as the federal requirement to warn of potential lead-based paint hazards in pre-1978 housing. A seller found to have knowingly lied about a defect may face legal penalties.

Discount Point: normally paid at closing and generally calculated to be equivalent to 1% of the total loan amount, discount points are paid to reduce the interest rate on a loan. In an ARM with an initial rate discount, the lender gives up a number of percentage points in interest to give you a lower rate and lower payments for part of the mortgage term (usually for one year or less). After the discount period, the ARM rate will probably go up depending on the index rate.

Down Payment: the portion of a home's purchase price that is paid in cash and is not part of the mortgage loan. This amount varies based on the loan type, but is determined by taking the difference of the sale price and the actual mortgage loan amount. Mortgage insurance is required when a down payment less than 20 percent is made.

Document Recording: after closing on a loan, certain documents are filed and made public record. Discharges for the prior mortgage holder are filed first. Then the deed is filed with the new owner's and mortgage company's names.

Due on Sale Clause: a provision of a loan allowing the lender to demand full repayment of the loan if the property is sold.

Duration: the number of years it will take to receive the present value of all future payments on a security to include both principal and interest.

Earnest Money (Deposit): money put down by a potential buyer to show that they are serious about purchasing the home; it becomes part of the down payment if the offer is accepted, is returned if the offer is rejected, or is forfeited if the buyer pulls out of the deal.

Earnings Per Share (EPS): a corporation's profit that is divided among each share of common stock. It is determined by taking the net earnings divided by the number of outstanding common stocks held. This is a way that a company reports profitability.

Easements: the legal rights that give someone other than the owner access to use property for a specific purpose. Easements may affect property values and are sometimes a part of the deed.

EEM: Energy Efficient Mortgage; an FHA program that helps homebuyers save money on utility bills by enabling them to finance the cost of adding energy efficiency features to a new or existing home as part of the home purchase.

Eminent Domain: when a government takes private property for public use. The owner receives payment for its fair market value. The property can then proceed to condemnation proceedings.

Encroachments: a structure that extends over the legal property line on to another individual's property. The property surveyor will note any encroachment on the lot survey done before property transfer. The person who owns the structure will be asked to remove it to prevent future problems.

Encumbrance: anything that affects title to a property, such as loans, leases, easements, or restrictions.

Equal Credit Opportunity Act (ECOA): a federal law requiring lenders to make credit available equally without discrimination based on race, color, religion, national origin, age, sex, marital status, or receipt of income from public assistance programs.

Equity: an owner's financial interest in a property; calculated by subtracting the amount still owed on the mortgage loon(s)from the fair market value of the property.

Escape Clause: a provision in a purchase contract that allows either party to cancel part or the entire contract if the other does not respond to changes to the sale within a set period. The most common use of the escape clause is if the buyer makes the purchase offer contingent on the sale of another house.

Escrow: funds held in an account to be used by the lender to pay for home insurance and property taxes. The funds may also be held by a third party until contractual conditions are met and then paid out.

Escrow Account: a separate account into which the lender puts a portion of each monthly mortgage payment; an escrow account provides the funds needed for such expenses as property taxes, homeowners insurance, mortgage insurance, etc.

Estate: the ownership interest of a person in real property. The sum total of all property, real and personal, owned by a person.

FICO Score: FICO is an abbreviation for Fair Isaac Corporation and refers to a person's credit score based on credit history. Lenders and credit card companies use the number to decide if the person is likely to pay his or her bills. A credit score is evaluated using information from the three major credit bureaus and is usually between 300 and 850.

FSBO (For Sale by Owner): a home that is offered for sale by the owner without the benefit of a real estate professional.

Fair Credit Reporting Act: federal act to ensure that credit bureaus are fair and accurate protecting the individual's privacy rights enacted in 1971 and revised in October 1997.

Fair Housing Act: a law that prohibits discrimination in all facets of the home buying process on the basis of race, color, national origin, religion, sex, familial status, or disability.

Fair Market Value: the hypothetical price that a willing buyer and seller will agree upon when they are acting freely, carefully, and with complete knowledge of the situation.

Familial Status: HUD uses this term to describe a single person, a pregnant woman or a household with children under 18 living with parents or legal custodians who might experience housing discrimination.

Fannie Mae: Federal National Mortgage Association (FNMA); a federally-chartered enterprise owned by private stockholders that purchases residential mortgages and converts them into securities for sale to investors; by purchasing mortgages, Fannie Mae supplies funds that lenders may loan to potential homebuyers. Also known as a Government Sponsored Enterprise (GSE).

FHA: Federal Housing Administration; established in 1934 to advance homeownership opportunities for all Americans; assists homebuyers by providing mortgage insurance to lenders to cover most losses that may occur when a borrower defaults; this encourages lenders to make loans to borrowers who might not qualify for conventional mortgages.

FHA TOTAL Mortgage Scorecard: The FHA TOTAL Mortgage Scorecard works with DU to process FHA single-family loan application and provide underwriting recommendations to help determine a loan's eligibility for insurance by FHA. The FHA Scorecard determines whether the borrower's credit and capacity for repayment of the mortgage appear to meet FHA guidelines, in which case the loan would receive an Approve recommendation, or whether the loan should be referred to a DE underwriter for further consideration and review.

First Mortgage: the mortgage with first priority if the loan is not paid.

Fixed Expenses: payments that do not vary from month to month.

Fixed-Rate Mortgage: a mortgage with payments that remain the same throughout the life of the loan because the interest rate and other terms are fixed and do not change.

Fixture: personal property permanently attached to real estate or real property that becomes a part of the real estate.

Float: the act of allowing an interest rate and discount points to fluctuate with changes in the market.

Flood Insurance: insurance that protects homeowners against losses from a flood; if a home is located in a flood plain, the lender will require flood insurance before approving a loan.

Forbearance: a lender may decide not to take legal action when a borrower is late in making a payment. Usually this occurs when a borrower sets up a plan that both sides agree will bring overdue mortgage payments up to date.

Foreclosure: a legal process in which mortgaged property is sold to pay the loan of the defaulting borrower. Foreclosure laws are based on the statutes of each state.

Freddie Mac: Federal Home Loan Mortgage Corporation (FHLM); a federally chartered corporation that purchases residential mortgages, securitizes them, and sells them to investors; this provides lenders with funds for new homebuyers. Also known as a Government Sponsored Enterprise (GSE).

Front End Ratio: a percentage comparing a borrower's total monthly cost to buy a house (mortgage principal and interest, insurance, and real estate taxes) to monthly income before deductions.

GSE: abbreviation for government sponsored enterprises: a collection of financial services corporations formed by the United States Congress to reduce interest rates for farmers and homeowners. Examples include Fannie Mae and Freddie Mac.

Ginnie Mae: Government National Mortgage Association (GNMA); a government-owned corporation overseen by the U.S. Department of Housing and Urban Development, Ginnie Mae pools FHA-insured and VA-guaranteed loans to back securities for private investment; as With Fannie Mae and Freddie Mac, the investment income provides funding that may then be lent to eligible borrowers by lenders.

Global Debt Facility: designed to allow investors all over the world to purchase debt (loans) of U.S. dollar and foreign currency through a variety of clearing systems.

Good Faith Estimate: an estimate of all closing fees including pre-paid and escrow items as well as lender charges; must be given to the borrower within three days after submission of a loan application.

Graduated Payment Mortgages: mortgages that begin with lower monthly payments that get slowly larger over a period of years, eventually reaching a fixed level and remaining there for the life of the loan. Graduated payment loans may be good if you expect your annual income to increase.

Grantee: an individual to whom an interest in real property is conveyed.

Grantor: an individual conveying an interest in real property.

Gross Income: money earned before taxes and other deductions. Sometimes it may include income from self-employment, rental property, alimony, child support, public assistance payments, and retirement benefits.

Guaranty Fee: payment to FannieMae from a lender for the assurance of timely principal and interest payments to MBS (Mortgage Backed Security) security holders.

HECM (Reverse Mortgage): the reverse mortgage is used by senior homeowners age 62 and older to convert the equity in their home into monthly streams of income and/or a line of credit to be repaid when they no longer occupy the home. A lending institution such as a mortgage lender, bank, credit union or savings and loan association funds the FHA insured loan, commonly known as HECM.

Hazard Insurance: protection against a specific loss, such as fire, wind etc., over a period of time that is secured by the payment of a regularly scheduled premium.

HELP: Homebuyer Education Learning Program; an educational program from the FHA that counsels people about the home buying process; HELP covers topics like budgeting, finding a home, getting a loan, and home maintenance; in most cases, completion of the program may entitle the homebuyer to a reduced initial FHA mortgage insurance premium-from 2.25% to 1.75% of the home purchase price.

Home Equity Line of Credit: a mortgage loan, usually in second mortgage, allowing a borrower to obtain cash against the equity of a home, up to a predetermined amount.

Home Equity Loan: a loan backed by the value of a home (real estate). If the borrower defaults or does not pay the loan, the lender has some rights to the property. The borrower can usually claim a home equity loan as a tax deduction. Home Inspection: an examination of the structure and mechanical systems to determine a home's quality, soundness and safety; makes the potential homebuyer aware of any repairs that may be needed. The homebuyer generally pays inspection fees.

Home Warranty: offers protection for mechanical systems and attached appliances against unexpected repairs not covered by homeowner's insurance; coverage extends over a specific time period and does not cover the home's structure.

Homeowner's Insurance: an insurance policy, also called hazard insurance, that combines protection against damage to a dwelling and its contents including fire, storms or other damages with protection against claims of negligence or inappropriate action that result in someone's injury or property damage. Most lenders require homeowners insurance and may escrow the cost. Flood insurance is generally not included in standard policies and must be purchased separately.

Homeownership Education Classes: classes that stress the need to develop a strong credit history and offer information about how to get a mortgage approved, qualify for a loan, choose an affordable home, go through financing and closing processes, and avoid mortgage problems that cause people to lose their homes.

Homestead Credit: property tax credit program, offered by some state governments, that provides reductions in property taxes to eligible households.

Housing Counseling Agency: provides counseling and assistance to individuals on a variety of issues, including loan default, fair housing, and home buying.

HUD: the U.S. Department of Housing and Urban Development; established in 1965, HUD works to create a decent home and suitable living environment for all Americans; it does this by addressing housing needs, improving and developing American communities, and enforcing fair housing laws.

HUD Handbooks & Mortgagee Letters: HUD Handbooks and Mortgagee Letters provide detailed processing instructions, and they advise the mortgage industry of major changes to FHA mortgage programs and procedures.

HUD1 Statement: also known as the "settlement sheet,"

or "closing statement" it itemizes all closing costs; must be given to the borrower at or before closing. Items that appear on the statement include real estate commissions, loan fees, points, and escrow amounts.

HVAC: Heating, Ventilation and Air Conditioning; a home's heating and cooling system.

Indemnification: to secure against any loss or damage, compensate or give security for reimbursement for loss or damage incurred. A homeowner should negotiate for inclusion of an indemnification provision in a contract with a general contractor or for a separate indemnity agreement protecting the homeowner from harm, loss or damage caused by actions or omissions of the general (and all sub) contractor.

Index: the measure of interest rate changes that the lender uses to decide how much the interest rate of an ARM will change over time. No one can be sure when an index rate will go up or down. If a lender bases interest rate adjustments on the average value of an index over time, your interest rate would not be as volatile. You should ask your lender how the index for any ARM you are considering has changed in recent years, and where it is reported.

Inflation: the number of dollars in circulation exceeds the amount of goods and services available for purchase; inflation results in a decrease in the dollar's value.

Inflation Coverage: endorsement to a homeowner's policy that automatically adjusts the amount of insurance to compensate for inflationary rises in the home's value. This type of coverage does not adjust for increases in the home's value due to improvements.

Inquiry: a credit report request. Each time a credit application is completed or more credit is requested counts as an inquiry. A large number of inquiries on a credit report can sometimes make a credit score lower.

Interest: a fee charged for the use of borrowing money.

Interest Rate: the amount of interest charged on a monthly loan payment, expressed as a percentage.

Interest Rate Swap: a transaction between two parties where each agrees to exchange payments tied to different interest rates for a specified period of time, generally based on a notional principal amount.

Intermediate Term Mortgage: a mortgage loan with a contractual maturity from the time of purchase equal to or less than 20 years.

Insurance: protection against a specific loss, such as fire,

wind etc., over a period of time that is secured by the payment of a regularly scheduled premium.

Joint Tenancy (with Rights of Survivorship): two or more owners share equal ownership and rights to the property. If a joint owner dies, his or her share of the property passes to the other owners, without probate. In joint tenancy, ownership of the property cannot be willed to someone who is not a joint owner.

Judgment: a legal decision; when requiring debt repayment, a judgment may include a property lien that secures the creditor's claim by providing a collateral source.

Jumbo Loan: or non-conforming loan, is a loan that exceeds Fannie Mae's and Freddie Mac's loan limits. Freddie Mac and Fannie Mae loans are referred to as conforming loans.

Late Payment Charges: the penalty the homeowner must pay when a mortgage payment is made after the due date grace period.

LDP: A Limited Denial of Participation (LDP) is an action taken by a HUD Field Office or the Deputy Assistant Secretary for Single Family (DASSF) or Multifamily (DASMF) Housing which excludes a party from further participation in a HUD program area.

Lease: a written agreement between a property owner and a tenant (resident) that stipulates the payment and conditions under which the tenant may occupy a home or apartment and states a specified period of time.

Lease Purchase (Lease Option): assists low to moderate income homebuyers in purchasing a home by allowing them to lease a home with an option to buy; the rent payment is made up of the monthly rental payment plus an additional amount that is credited to an account for use as a down payment.

Lender: A term referring to an person or company that makes loans for real estate purchases. Sometimes referred to as a loan officer or lender.

Lender Option Commitments: an agreement giving a lender the option to deliver loans or securities by a certain date at agreed upon terms.

Liabilities: a person's financial obligations such as long-term / short-term debt, and other financial obligations to be paid.

Liability Insurance: insurance coverage that protects against claims alleging a property owner's negligence or action resulted in bodily injury or damage to another person. It is normally included in homeowner's insurance policies.

Lien: a legal claim against property that must be satisfied when the property is sold. A claim of money against a property, wherein the value of the property is used as security in repayment of a debt. Examples include a mechanic's lien, which might be for the unpaid cost of building supplies, or a tax lien for unpaid property taxes. A lien is a defect on the title and needs to be settled before transfer of ownership. A lien release is a written report of the settlement of a lien and is recorded in the public record as evidence of payment.

Lien Waiver: A document that releases a consumer (homeowner) from any further obligation for payment of a debt once it has been paid in full. Lien waivers typically are used by homeowners who hire a contractor to provide work and materials to prevent any subcontractors or suppliers of materials from filing a lien against the homeowner for nonpayment.

Life Cap: a limit on the range interest rates can increase or decrease over the life of an adjustable-rate mortgage (ARM).

Line of Credit: an agreement by a financial institution such as a bank to extend credit up to a certain amount for a certain time to a specified borrower.

Liquid Asset: a cash asset or an asset that is easily converted into cash.

Listing Agreement: a contract between a seller and a real estate professional to market and sell a home. A listing agreement obligates the real estate professional (or his or her agent) to seek qualified buyers, report all purchase offers and help negotiate the highest possible price and most favorable terms for the property seller.

Loan: money borrowed that is usually repaid with interest.

Loan Acceleration: an acceleration clause in a loan document is a statement in a mortgage that gives the lender the right to demand payment of the entire outstanding balance if a monthly payment is missed.

Loan Fraud: purposely giving incorrect information on a loan application in order to better qualify for a loan; may result in civil liability or criminal penalties.

Loan Officer: a representative of a lending or mortgage company who is responsible for soliciting homebuyers, qualifying and processing of loans. They may also be called lender, loan representative, account executive or loan rep.

Loan Origination Fee: a charge by the lender to cover the administrative costs of making the mortgage. This charge is paid at the closing and varies with the lender and type of loan. A loan origination fee of 1 to 2 percent of the mortgage amount is common.

Loan Servicer: the company that collects monthly mortgage payments and disperses property taxes and insurance payments. Loan servicers also monitor nonperforming loans, contact delinquent borrowers, and notify insurers and investors of potential problems. Loan servicers may be the lender or a specialized company that just handles loan servicing under contract with the lender or the investor who owns the loan.

Loan to Value (LTV) Ratio: a percentage calculated by dividing the amount borrowed by the price or appraised value of the home to be purchased; the higher the LTV, the less cash a borrower is required to pay as down payment.

Lock-In: since interest rates can change frequently, many lenders offer an interest rate lock-in that guarantees a specific interest rate if the loan is closed within a specific time.

Lock-in Period: the length of time that the lender has guaranteed a specific interest rate to a borrower.

Loss Mitigation: a process to avoid foreclosure; the lender tries to help a borrower who has been unable to make loan payments and is in danger of defaulting on his or her loan

Mandatory Delivery Commitment: an agreement that a lender will deliver loans or securities by a certain date at agreed-upon terms.

Margin: the number of percentage points the lender adds to the index rate to calculate the ARM interest rate at each adjustment.

Market Value: the amount a willing buyer would pay a willing seller for a home. An appraised value is an estimate of the current fair market value.

Maturity: the date when the principal balance of a loan becomes due and payable.

Median Price: the price of the house that falls in the middle of the total number of homes for sale in that area.

Medium Term Notes: unsecured general obligations of Fannie Mae with maturities of one day or more and with principal and interest payable in U.S. dollars.

Merged Credit Report: raw data pulled from two or

more of the major credit-reporting firms.

Mitigation: term usually used to refer to various changes or improvements made in a home; for instance, to reduce the average level of radon.

Modification: when a lender agrees to modify the terms of a mortgage without refinancing the loan.

Mortgage: a lien on the property that secures the Promise to repay a loan. A security agreement between the lender and the buyer in which the property is collateral for the loan. The mortgage gives the lender the right to collect payment on the loan and to foreclose if the loan obligations are not met.

Mortgage Acceleration Clause: a clause allowing a lender, under certain circumstances, demand the entire balance of a loan is repaid in a lump sum. The acceleration clause is usually triggered if the home is sold, title to the property is changed, the loan is refinanced or the borrower defaults on a scheduled payment.

Mortgage-Backed Security (MBS): a Fannie Mae security that represents an undivided interest in a group of mortgages. Principal and interest payments from the individual mortgage loans are grouped and paid out to the MBS holders.

Mortgage Banker: a company that originates loans and resells them to secondary mortgage lenders like Fannie Mae or Freddie Mac.

Mortgage Broker: a firm that originates and processes loans for a number of lenders.

Mortgage Credit Analysis Worksheet (MCAW): The worksheet that an underwriter uses to analyze and summarize the mortgage transaction for an FHA loan. The underwriter is required to review and make changes to the Mortgage Credit Analysis Worksheet, to indicate the loan recommendation on the form, and to insert their CHUMS ID with the decision date. If DU returns an underwriting recommendation of Approve/Eligible, the underwriter will insert the applicable CHUMS ID assigned to the lender by HUD for system approvals.

Mortgage Life and Disability Insurance: term life insurance bought by borrowers to pay off a mortgage in the event of death or make monthly payments in the case of disability. The amount of coverage decreases as the principal balance declines. There are many different terms of coverage determining amounts of payments and when payments begin and end.

Mortgage Insurance: a policy that protects lenders against some or most of the losses that can occur when a borrower defaults on a mortgage loan; mortgage insurance is required primarily for borrowers with a down payment of less than 20% of the home's purchase price.

Mortgage Insurance Premium (MIP): a monthly payment -usually part of the mortgage payment - paid by a borrower for mortgage insurance.

Mortgage Interest Deduction: the interest cost of a mortgage, which is a tax-deductible expense. The interest reduces the taxable income of taxpayers.

Mortgage Modification: a loss mitigation option that allows a borrower to refinance and/or extend the term of the mortgage loan and thus reduce the monthly payments.

Mortgage Note: a legal document obligating a borrower to repay a loan at a stated interest rate during a specified period; the agreement is secured by a mortgage that is recorded in the public records along with the deed.

Mortgage Qualifying Ratio: Used to calculate the maximum amount of funds that an individual traditionally may be able to afford. A typical mortgage qualifying ratio is 28/36.

Mortgage Score: a score based on a combination of information about the borrower that is obtained from the loan application, the credit report, and property value information. The score is a comprehensive analysis of the borrower's ability to repay a mortgage loan and manage credit.

Mortgagee: the lender in a mortgage agreement. Mortgagor - The borrower in a mortgage agreement.

Mortgagor: the borrower in a mortgage agreement.

Multifamily Housing: a building with more than four residential rental units.

Multiple Listing Service (MLS): within the Metro Columbus area, Realtors submit listings and agree to attempt to sell all properties in the MLS. The MLS is a service of the local Columbus Board of Realtors®. The local MLS has a protocol for updating listings and sharing commissions. The MLS offers the advantage of more timely information, availability, and access to houses and other types of property on the market.

National Credit Repositories: currently, there are three companies that maintain national credit - reporting databases. These are Equifax, Experian, and Trans Union, referred to as Credit Bureaus.

Negative Amortization: amortization means that monthly payments are large enough to pay the interest and reduce the principal on your mortgage. Negative amortization occurs when the monthly payments do not cover all of the interest cost. The interest cost that isn't covered is added to the unpaid principal balance. This means that even after making many payments, you could owe more than you did at the beginning of the loan. Negative amortization can occur when an ARM has a payment cap that results in monthly payments not high enough to cover the interest due.

Net Income: Your take-home pay, the amount of money that you receive in your paycheck after taxes and deductions.

No Cash Out Refinance: a refinance of an existing loan only for the amount remaining on the mortgage. The borrower does not get any cash against the equity of the home. Also called a "rate and term refinance."

No Cost Loan: there are many variations of a no cost loan. Generally, it is a loan that does not charge for items such as title insurance, escrow fees, settlement fees, appraisal, recording fees or notary fees. It may also offer no points. This lessens the need for upfront cash during the buying process however no cost loans have a higher interest rate.

Nonperforming Asset: an asset such as a mortgage that is not currently accruing interest or which interest is not being paid.

Note: a legal document obligating a borrower to repay a mortgage loan at a stated interest rate over a specified period of time.

Note Rate: the interest rate stated on a mortgage note.

Notice of Default: a formal written notice to a borrower that there is a default on a loan and that legal action is possible.

Notional Principal Amount: the proposed amount which interest rate swap payments are based but generally not paid or received by either party.

Non-Conforming loan: is a loan that exceeds Fannie Mae's and Freddie Mac's loan limits. Freddie Mac and Fannie Mae loans are referred to as conforming loans.

Notary Public: a person who serves as a public official and certifies the authenticity of required signatures on a document by signing and stamping the document.

Offer: indication by a potential buyer of a willingness to purchase a home at a specific price; generally put forth in writing.

Original Principal Balance: the total principal owed on a mortgage prior to any payments being made.

Origination: the process of preparing, submitting, and evaluating a loan application; generally includes a credit check, verification of employment, and a property appraisal.

Origination Fee: the charge for originating a loan; is usually calculated in the form of points and paid at closing. One point equals one percent of the loan amount. On a conventional loan, the loan origination fee is the number of points a borrower pays.

Owner Financing: a home purchase where the seller provides all or part of the financing, acting as a lender.

Ownership: ownership is documented by the deed to a property. The type or form of ownership is important if there is a change in the status of the owners or if the property changes ownership.

Owner's Policy: the insurance policy that protects the buyer from title defects.

PITI: Principal, Interest, Taxes, and Insurance: the four elements of a monthly mortgage payment; payments of principal and interest go directly towards repaying the loan while the portion that covers taxes and insurance (homeowner's and mortgage, if applicable) goes into an escrow account to cover the fees when they are due.

PITI Reserves: a cash amount that a borrower must have on hand after making a down payment and paying all closing costs for the purchase of a home. The principal, interest, taxes, and insurance (PITI) reserves must equal the amount that the borrower would have to pay for PITI for a predefined number of months.

PMI: Private Mortgage Insurance; privately-owned companies that offer standard and special affordable mortgage insurance programs for qualified borrowers with down payments of less than 20% of a purchase price.

Partial Claim: a loss mitigation option offered by the FHA that allows a borrower, with help from a lender, to get an interest-free loan from HUD to bring their mortgage payments up to date.

Partial Payment: a payment that is less than the total amount owed on a monthly mortgage payment. Normally, lenders do not accept partial payments. The lender may make exceptions during times of difficulty. Contact your lender prior to the due date if a partial payment is needed.

Payment Cap: a limit on how much an ARM's payment may increase, regardless of how much the interest rate increases.

Payment Change Date: the date when a new monthly payment amount takes effect on an adjustable-rate mortgage (ARM) or a graduated-payment mortgage (GPM). Generally, the payment change date occurs in the month immediately after the interest rate adjustment date.

Payment Due Date: Contract language specifying when payments are due on money borrowed. The due date is always indicated and means that the payment must be received on or before the specified date. Grace periods prior to assessing a late fee or additional interest do not eliminate the responsibility of making payments on time.

Perils: for homeowner's insurance, an event that can damage the property. Homeowner's insurance may cover the property for a wide variety of perils caused by accidents, nature, or people.

Personal Property: any property that is not real property or attached to real property. For example furniture is not attached however a new light fixture would be considered attached and part of the real property.

Planned Unit Development (PUD): a development that is planned, and constructed as one entity. Generally, there are common features in the homes or lots governed by covenants attached to the deed. Most planned developments have common land and facilities owned and managed by the owner's or neighborhood association. Homeowners usually are required to participate in the association via a payment of annual dues.

Points: a point is equal to one percent of the principal amount of your mortgage. For example, if you get a mortgage for $95,000, one point means you pay $950 to the lender. Lenders frequently charge points in both fixed-rate and adjustable-rate mortgages in order to increase the yield on the mortgage and to cover loan closing costs. These points usually are collected at closing and may be paid by the borrower or the home seller, or may be split between them.

Power of Attorney: a legal document that authorizes another person to act on your behalf. A power of attorney can grant complete authority or can be limited to certain acts or certain periods of time or both.

Pre-Approval: a lender commits to lend to a potential borrower a fixed loan amount based on a completed loan application, credit reports, debt, savings and has been reviewed by an underwriter. The commitment remains as long as the borrower still meets the qualification requirements at the time of purchase. This does not guaranty a loan until the property has passed inspections underwriting guidelines.

Predatory Lending: abusive lending practices that include a mortgage loan to someone who does not have the ability to repay. It also pertains to repeated refinancing of a loan charging high interest and fees each time.

Predictive Variables: The variables that are part of the formula comprising elements of a credit-scoring model. These variables are used to predict a borrower's future credit performance.

Preferred Stock: stock that takes priority over common stock with regard to dividends and liquidation rights. Preferred stockholders typically have no voting rights.

Pre-foreclosure Sale: a procedure in which the borrower is allowed to sell a property for an amount less than what is owed on it to avoid a foreclosure. This sale fully satisfies the borrower's debt.

Prepayment: any amount paid to reduce the principal balance of a loan before the due date or payment in full of a mortgage. This can occur with the sale of the property, the pay off the loan in full, or a foreclosure. In each case, full payment occurs before the loan has been fully amortized.

Prepayment Penalty: a provision in some loans that charge a fee to a borrower who pays off a loan before it is due.

Pre-Foreclosure sale: allows a defaulting borrower to sell the mortgaged property to satisfy the loan and avoid foreclosure.

Pre-Qualify: a lender informally determines the maximum amount an individual is eligible to borrow. This is not a guaranty of a loan.

Premium: an amount paid on a regular schedule by a policyholder that maintains insurance coverage.

Prepayment: payment of the mortgage loan before the scheduled due date; may be Subject to a prepayment penalty.

Prepayment Penalty: a fee charged to a homeowner who pays one or more monthly payments before the due date. It can also apply to principal reduction payments.

Prepayment Penalty Mortgage (PPM): a type of mortgage that requires the borrower to pay a penalty for prepayment, partial payment of principal or for repaying the entire loan within a certain time period. A partial payment is generally defined as an amount exceeding 20% of the original principal balance.

Price Range: the high and low amount a buyer is willing to pay for a home.

Prime Rate: the interest rate that banks charge to preferred customers. Changes in the prime rate are publicized in the business media. Prime rate can be used as the basis for adjustable rate mortgages (ARMs) or home equity lines of credit. The prime rate also affects the current interest rates being offered at a particular point in time on fixed mortgages. Changes in the prime rate do not affect the interest on a fixed mortgage.

Principal: the amount of money borrowed to buy a house or the amount of the loan that has not been paid back to the lender. This does not include the interest paid to borrow that money. The principal balance is the amount owed on a loan at any given time. It is the original loan amount minus the total repayments of principal made.

Principal, Interest, Taxes, and Insurance (PITI): the four elements of a monthly mortgage payment; payments of principal and interest go directly towards repaying the loan while the portion that covers taxes and insurance (homeowner's and mortgage, if applicable) goes into an escrow account to cover the fees when they are due.

Private Mortgage Insurance (PMI): insurance purchased by a buyer to protect the lender in the event of default. The cost of mortgage insurance is usually added to the monthly payment. Mortgage insurance is generally maintained until over 20 Percent of the outstanding amount of the loan is paid or for a set period of time, seven years is normal. Mortgage insurance may be available through a government agency, such as the Federal Housing Administration (FHA) or the Veterans Administration (VA), or through private mortgage insurance companies (PMI).

Promissory Note: a written promise to repay a specified amount over a specified period of time.

Property (Fixture and Non-Fixture): in a real estate contract, the property is the land within the legally described boundaries and all permanent structures and fixtures. Ownership of the property confers the legal right to use the property as allowed within the law and within the restrictions of zoning or easements. Fixture property refers to those items permanently attached to the structure, such as carpeting or a ceiling fan, which transfers with the property.

Property Tax: a tax charged by local government and used to fund municipal services such as schools, police, or street maintenance. The amount of property tax is determined locally by a formula, usually based on a percent per $1,000 of assessed value of the property.

Property Tax Deduction: the U.S. tax code allows homeowners to deduct the amount they have paid in property taxes from there total income.

Public Record Information: Court records of events that are a matter of public interest such as credit, bankruptcy, foreclosure and tax liens. The presence of public record information on a credit report is regarded negatively by creditors.

Punch List: a list of items that have not been completed at the time of the final walk through of a newly constructed home.

Purchase Offer: A detailed, written document that makes an offer to purchase a property, and that may be amended several times in the process of negotiations. When signed by all parties involved in the sale, the purchase offer becomes a legally binding contract, sometimes called the Sales Contract.

Qualifying Ratios: guidelines utilized by lenders to determine how much money a homebuyer is qualified to borrow. Lending guidelines typically include a maximum housing expense to income ratio and a maximum monthly expense to income ratio.

Quitclaim Deed: a deed transferring ownership of a property but does not make any guarantee of clear title.

RESPA: Real Estate Settlement Procedures Act; a law protecting consumers from abuses during the residential real estate purchase and loan process by requiring lenders to disclose all settlement costs, practices, and relationships.

Radon: a radioactive gas found in some homes that, if occurring in strong enough concentrations, can cause health problems.

Rate Cap: a limit on an ARM on how much the interest rate or mortgage payment may change. Rate caps limit how much the interest rates can rise or fall on the adjustment dates and over the life of the loan.

Rate Lock: a commitment by a lender to a borrower guaranteeing a specific interest rate over a period of time at a set cost.

Real Estate Agent: an individual who is licensed to negotiate and arrange real estate sales; works for a real estate broker.

Real Estate Mortgage Investment Conduit (REMIC): a security representing an interest in a trust having multiple classes of securities. The securities of each class entitle investors to cash payments structured differently from the payments on the underlying mortgages.

Real Estate Property Tax Deduction: a tax deductible expense reducing a taxpayer's taxable income.

Real Estate Settlement Procedures Act (RESPA): a law protecting consumers from abuses during the residential real estate purchase and loan process by requiring lenders to disclose all settlement costs, practices, and relationships.

Real Property: land, including all the natural resources and permanent buildings on it.

Recorder: the public official who keeps records of transactions concerning real property. Sometimes known as a "Registrar of Deeds" or "County Clerk."

Recording: the recording in a registrar's office of an executed legal document. These include deeds, mortgages, satisfaction of a mortgage, or an extension of a mortgage making it a part of the public record.

Recording Fees: charges for recording a deed with the appropriate government agency.

Refinancing: paying off one loan by obtaining another; refinancing is generally done to secure better loan terms (like a lower interest rate).

Rehabilitation Mortgage: a mortgage that covers the costs of rehabilitating (repairing or Improving) a property; some rehabilitation mortgages - like the FHA's 203(k) - allow a borrower to roll the costs of rehabilitation and home purchase into one mortgage loan.

Reinstatement Period: a phase of the foreclosure process where the homeowner has an opportunity to stop the foreclosure by paying money that is owed to the lender.

Remaining Balance: the amount of principal that has not yet been repaid.

Remaining Term: the original amortization term minus the number of payments that have been applied.

Repayment plan: an agreement between a lender and a delinquent borrower where the borrower agrees to make additional payments to pay down past due amounts while making regularly scheduled payments.

Return On Average Common Equity: net income available to common stockholders, as a percentage of average common stockholder equity.

Reverse Mortgage (HECM): the reverse mortgage is used by senior homeowners age 62 and older to convert the equity in their home into monthly streams of income and/or a line of credit to be repaid when they no longer occupy the home. A lending institution such as a mortgage lender, bank, credit union or savings and loan association funds the FHA insured loan, commonly known as HECM.

Right of First Refusal: a provision in an agreement that requires the owner of a property to give one party an opportunity to purchase or lease a property before it is offered for sale or lease to others.

Risk Based Capital: an amount of capital needed to offset losses during a ten-year period with adverse circumstances.

Risk Based Pricing: Fee structure used by creditors based on risks of granting credit to a borrower with a poor credit history.

Risk Scoring: an automated way to analyze a credit report verses a manual review. It takes into account late payments, outstanding debt, credit experience, and number of inquiries in an unbiased manner.

Sale Leaseback: when a seller deeds property to a buyer for a payment, and the buyer simultaneously leases the property back to the seller.

Second Mortgage: an additional mortgage on property. In case of a default the first mortgage must be paid before the second mortgage. Second loans are more risky for the lender and usually carry a higher interest rate.

Secondary Mortgage Market: the buying and selling of mortgage loans. Investors purchase residential mortgages originated by lenders, which in turn provides the lenders with capital for additional lending.

Secured Loan: a loan backed by collateral such as property.

Security: the property that will be pledged as collateral for a loan.

Seller Take Back: an agreement where the owner of a property provides second mortgage financing. These are often combined with an assumed mortgage instead of a portion of the seller's equity.

Serious Delinquency: a mortgage that is 90 days or more past due.

Servicer: a business that collects mortgage payments from borrowers and manages the borrower's escrow accounts.

Servicing: the collection of mortgage from borrowers and related responsibilities of a loan servicer.

Setback: the distance between a property line and the area where building can take place. Setbacks are used to assure space between buildings and from roads for a many of purposes including drainage and utilities.

Settlement: another name for closing.

Settlement Statement: a document required by the Real Estate Settlement Procedures Act (RESPA). It is an itemized statement of services and charges relating to the closing of a property transfer. The buyer has the right to examine the settlement statement 1 day before the closing. This is called the HUD-1 Settlement Statement.

Special Forbearance: a loss mitigation option where the lender arranges a revised repayment plan for the borrower that may include a temporary reduction or suspension of monthly loan payments.

Stockholders' Equity: the sum of proceeds from the issuance of stock and retained earnings less amounts paid to repurchase common shares.

Stripped MBS (SMBS): securities created by "stripping" or separating the principal and interest payments from the underlying pool of mortgages into two classes of securities, with each receiving a different proportion of the principal and interest payments.

Sub-Prime Loan: "B" Loan or "B" paper with FICO scores from 620 - 659. "C" Loan or "C" Paper with FICO scores typically from 580 to 619. An industry term to used to describe loans with less stringent lending and underwriting terms and conditions. Due to the higher risk, sub-prime loans charge higher interest rates and fees.

Subordinate: to place in a rank of lesser importance or to make one claim secondary to another.

Survey: a property diagram that indicates legal boundaries, easements, encroachments, rights of way, improvement locations, etc. Surveys are conducted by licensed surveyors and are normally required by the lender in order to confirm that the property boundaries and features such as buildings, and easements are correctly described in the legal description of the property.

Sweat Equity: using labor to build or improve a property as part of the down payment.

Third Party Origination: a process by which a lender uses another party to completely or partially originate, process, underwrite, close, fund, or package the mortgages it plans to deliver to the secondary mortgage market.

Terms: The period of time and the interest rate agreed upon by the lender and the borrower to repay a loan.

Title: a legal document establishing the right of ownership and is recorded to make it part of the public record. Also known as a Deed.

Title 1: an FHA-insured loan that allows a borrower to make non-luxury improvements (like renovations or repairs) to their home; Title I loans less than $7,500 don't require a property lien.

Title Company: a company that specializes in examining and insuring titles to real estate.

Title Defect: an outstanding claim on a property that limits the ability to sell the property. Also referred to as a cloud on the title.

Title Insurance: insurance that protects the lender against any claims that arise from arguments about ownership of the property; also available for homebuyers. An insurance policy guaranteeing the accuracy of a title search protecting against errors. Most lenders require the buyer to purchase title insurance protecting the lender against loss in the event of a title defect. This charge is included in the closing costs. A policy that protects the buyer from title defects is known as an owner's policy and requires an additional charge.

Title Search: a check of public records to be sure that the seller is the recognized owner of the real estate and that there are no unsettled liens or other claims against the property.

Transfer of Ownership: any means by which ownership of a property changes hands. These include purchase of a property, assumption of mortgage debt, exchange of possession of a property via a land sales contract or any other land trust device.

Transfer Taxes: State and local taxes charged for the transfer of real estate. Usually equal to a percentage of the sales price.

Treasury Index: can be used as the basis for adjustable rate mortgages (ARMs) It is based on the results of auctions that the U.S. Treasury holds for its Treasury bills and securities.

Truth-in-Lending: a federal law obligating a lender to give full written disclosure of all fees, terms, and conditions associated with the loan initial period and then adjusts to another rate that lasts for the term of the loan.

Two Step Mortgage: an adjustable-rate mortgage (ARM) that has one interest rate for the first five to seven years of its term and adifferent interest rate for the remainder of the term.

Trustee: a person who holds or controls property for the benefit of another.

Underwriting: the process of analyzing a loan

application to determine the amount of risk involved in making the loan; it includes a review of the potential borrower's credit history and a judgment of the property value.

Uniform Case Binder: After the lender underwrites and closes the loan, lenders must submit information about the loan, organized in a Case Binder in an FHA required stacking order. The FHA Case Binder is a subset of the lender's "loan file" and is sent to a HUD Home Ownership Center where reviewers and endorsement clerks check the paperwork to determine if the mortgage meets the eligibility requirements for insurance and that all required documents and signatures are present. If there is a discrepancy, the endorsement clerk may reject the binder and issue a Notice of Return (NOR) to the lender.

Up Front Charges: the fees charged to homeowners by the lender at the time of closing a mortgage loan. This includes points, broker's fees, insurance, and other charges.

VA (Department of Veterans Affairs): a federal agency, which guarantees loans made to veterans; similar to mortgage insurance, a loan guarantee protects lenders against loss that may result from a borrower default.

VA Mortgage: a mortgage guaranteed by the Department of Veterans Affairs (VA).

Variable Expenses: Costs or payments that may vary from month to month, for example, gasoline or food.

Variance: a special exemption of a zoning law to allow the property to be used in a manner different from an existing law.

Vested: a point in time when you may withdraw funds from an investment account, such as a retirement account, without penalty.

Warranty Deed: a legal document that includes the guarantee the seller is the true owner of the property, has the right to sell the property and there are no claims against the
property.

Zoning: local laws established to control the uses of land within a particular area. Zoning laws are used to separate residential land from areas of non-residential use, such as industry or businesses. Zoning ordinances include many provisions governing such things as type of structure, setbacks, lot size, and uses of a building.

Made in the USA
Lexington, KY
14 October 2016